P9-DIY-452

YEARBOOK

2005

The Best & Worst of the Year

Super heroes: Dana and Christopher Reeve five years before his sudden death.

All happy families are alike; each unhappy family is unhappy in its own way. Leo Tolstoy, in the opening lines of *Anna Karenina*, his 1876 novel that went to No. 1 on the bestseller list after being picked for Oprah's Book Club

You'd be amazed at the number of people who want to introduce themselves to you in the men's room. John Kerry, on Comedy Central, about campaign life

your s--- Madonna, revealing her mothering mantra on *20/20*

We want the very, very best and the very, very worst.

Nigel Lithgoe, *American Idol* executive producer, on auditions for the show

In Hollywood, I see many starving people every day. We call them actresses. Ironically, when offered food, they decline. *Will & Grace*'s Sean Hayes

I could argue with this spoon, and it would be the same as arguing with you.

Nick Lachey to Jessica Simpson on *Newlyweds*

Being on at a time when people can see me. My parents have no idea what I do for a living. They think I'm still in law school. Conan O'Brien, on the benefits of taking over *The Tonight Show* in 2009

heaven; go everywhere. Sharon Stone

Never been arrested. All the child-star clichés.

Macaulay Culkin, now 24, three months before he was busted for pot possession

Nothing screams rock star like a Toyota Prius.

Sheryl Crow

Fame is addictive. Money is addictive. Attention is addictive. But golf is second to none.

Marc Anthony, after marrying Jennifer Lopez and buying a $22,000 set of Honma irons from Japan

Editor **RICHARD SANDERS** Creative Director **RINA MIGLIACCIO** Art Director **PETER B. CURY** Senior Editor **RICHARD BURGHEIM** Picture Editor **BRIAN BELOVITCH** Writers **STEVE DOUGHERTY, LISA RUSSELL, KYLE SMITH, CHRIS STRAUSS** Reporters **RANDY VEST** (Chief), **MELINDA DODD, RENNIE DYBALL, ANNE HOLLISTER, DEBRA LEWIS, JENNIFER SOBIE** Copy Chief **TOMMY DUNNE** Production Artist **MICHAEL APONTE** Administrative Assistant **PATRICIA HUSTOO**

SPECIAL THANKS to Luciana Chang (Photo Dept.) and to the PEOPLE Research Library: Robert Britton (Director), Céline Wojtala (Deputy), Jane Bealer, Sal Covarrúbias, Margery Frohlinger, Charles Nelson, Susan Radlauer, Annette Rusin, Ean Sheehy, Jack Styczynski, Patrick Yang

TIME INC. HOME ENTERTAINMENT President **ROB GURSHA** Vice President, New Product Development **RICHARD FRAIMAN** Executive Director, Marketing Services **CAROL PITTARD** Director, Retail & Special Sales **TOM MIFSUD** Director of Finance **TRICIA GRIFFIN** Prepress Manager **EMILY RABIN** Associate Book Production Manager **SUZANNE JANSO** Associate Product Manager **TAYLOR GREENE**

SPECIAL THANKS to Bozena Bannett, Alexandra Bliss, Bernadette Corbie, Robert Dente, Anne-Michelle Gallero, Peter Harper, Robert Marasco, Natalie McCrea, Brooke McGuire, Jonathan Polsky, Margarita Quiogue, Mary Jane Rigoroso, Steven Sandonato

Published by People Books; Time Inc., 1271 Avenue of the Americas, New York, New York 10020. All rights reserved. No part of this book may be reproduced in any form or by any electronic or mechanical means, including information storage and retrieval systems, without permission in writing from the publisher, except by a reviewer, who may quote brief passages in a review. ISBN: 1-932273-51-4. ISSN: 1522-5895. People Books is a trademark of Time Inc. We welcome your comments and suggestions about People Books. Please write to us at: People Books, Attention: Book Editors, PO Box 11016, Des Moines, IA 50336-1016. If you would like to order any of our hardcover Collector's Edition books, please call us at 1-800-327-6388 (Monday through Friday 7:00 a.m.–8:00 p.m. or Saturday 7:00 a.m.–6:00 p.m. Central Time). Copyright © 2005 Time Inc. Home Entertainment.

THE BEST&WORST OF THE YEAR

Between the *Passion* of Mel and the peekaboo skirts of Paris, we were riveted by Bush and Kerry, shocked by Janet and Tara, wowed by Law and Lohan, entertained by Foxx, awed by the Sox and hooked on iPods

After doffing his lucky Red Sox cap and double-checking Ohio, Kerry told supporters, "We cannot win this election."

THE PEOPLE SPOKE, LOUDLY

"The race," said Dan Rather on election night, "is hotter than a Times Square Rolex." The embattled CBS anchor, who hadn't exactly enjoyed his own walk-on role in one of the most impassioned and acrimonious campaign dramas in memory, certainly called that one right. After months of dueling claims and alleged flip-flops, the candidates found themselves in a cliffhanger that wasn't resolved until the next day, when John Kerry, standing in for the fat lady, made a phone call beginning "Congratulations, Mr. President."

With that, George W. Bush, 58, had, unlike his father, won a second term. And, unlike in 2000, he'd won with a popular-vote plurality, one exceeding 3 million. The turnout represented an all-time record and, percentage-wise, the highest since 1968. Though spurred in part by a get-out-the-youth effort—P. Diddy's Vote or Die drive and the Bruce Springsteen-led Vote for Change tour—the most galvanized were those who supported the stay-the-course ticket. Values issues like the definition of marriage or stem-cell research or gun control seemed to outweigh economic concerns. And problems in Iraq aside, Americans felt more secure retaining the Commander in Chief who had rallied the nation with a bullhorn at Ground Zero on 9/14.

On the stump, Bush proved a warmer, happier warrior than his opponent, just as his wife, Laura, 58, came off as more down-home than the Mozambique-born Teresa Heinz Kerry, 66. The Bush twins, Barbara and Jenna, 21, fresh out of college and natural cheerleaders as Dad had been in school, campaigned for the first time. The loser, Kerry, 61, would return as a senator from Massachusetts. Running mate John Edwards, 51, would go home to North Carolina with his wife, Elizabeth, 55, who was diagnosed with breast cancer the afternoon of the Democratic concession. For bit players like the Kerry-attacking Swift Boat Veterans for Truth and the disgruntled Texan whose forged documents Rather presented on *60 Minutes* as proof that Bush had shirked his National Guard duty, the election meant a slow fade into history. "America has spoken," said Bush, reaching out in his victory remarks to the millions suffering those blue-state blues. "With that trust comes a duty to serve all Americans, and I will do my best to fulfill that duty every day as your President."

"I take that as a compliment," Bush said on election day when asked about the divisive passions he inspires. "It means I'm willing to take a stand."

SLICKEST SOUL MAN

The declaration that "what I say goes, and I'm in control" pushed his single "My Way" to No. 2 on the *Billboard* charts in 1998, but it wasn't until 2004 and the release of *Confessions* that **Usher**'s boast became reality. The album enjoyed the biggest debut by a male R&B artist in history, selling 1.1 million copies in its first week and eventually passing 7 million. Usher Raymond IV, a phenom from age 14, had finally at 26 set himself apart from his R&B peers, cowriting nine songs on *Confessions,* mixing cryptically soulful slow jams and hip-hop-inspired club hits like the ubiquitous chart topper "Yeah!" Sales were also pumped by his high-profile breakup with longtime love Rozonda "Chilli" Thomas of TLC and fans' incorrect assumption that the lyrics were autobiographical. "Not one song on the album is about me or our relationship," Thomas noted. Usher had elsewhere admitted to damaging the relationship with his infidelity.

Not that he didn't enjoy the rebound, playfully advertising his new single status to Halle Berry and Lucy Liu in a PEOPLE interview. He may have failed to land Catwoman or the Charlie's Angel, but he did manage to squire supermodel Naomi Campbell after exchanging numbers the weekend of the MTV Video Awards in Miami. In the summer, Usher left his Atlanta base to tour behind his album in a bus, a $750,000 rolling bachelor pad equipped with plasma TV, five beds, workout space and a granite-tiled shower, embodying his byword "The sky's the limit." That goes for his career too. The Grammy winner has launched his own record label and debit card as well as an acting career that may include starring in a biopic of his hero Marvin Gaye. "I've got a lot of plans," he explained. "I've got one of those minds that never clicks off."

"I don't believe in good luck," the chart-saturating artist proclaimed. "I believe in blessings."

MOST SHAMELESS REUNION

A few days after her release from a Washington State prison, 42-year-old ex-teacher **Mary Kay Letourneau** told a friend, "I'm in shell shock—I feel like the *Quantum Leap* guy." Understandable: Vili Fualaau, the former student she began sleeping with when he was 12, was now 21 and ready to marry her. Their two daughters—the youngest the result of the illegal backseat rendezvous that forced the paroled sex offender back to prison in 1998—were now 7 and 6. Even Letourneau had softened a bit. While she viewed her relationship with Fualaau as "a true union of bodies and souls," she now regrets the devastating consequences for her four older kids, now 10 to 19 and living with her ex, Steve. "She wants to make things right for them," said friend Christina Dress. "They've been through a lot." Reconciliation may be easier said than done. "I feel like we kind of missed out on a lot of stuff," said son Steve Jr., "because of the bad decision she made."

Fualaau (left), professing his love for Letourneau (right), said, "We still have the same feelings for each other—times forever."

MOST STUDIED STUDENT

Even for someone who's been appearing on-camera since her debut as *Full House*'s precocious Michelle Tanner (along with twin sister Ashley) at just 9 months old, the crush of media attention during her first year of adulthood must have seemed super-intense for **Mary-Kate Olsen.** America's closest real-life versions of the Jim Carrey character in *The Truman Show,* the Olsen twins had been somehow able to combine lovable onscreen personalities and business savvy with solid grounding. "To be under the microscope like they have been is tough," said *Full House* costar Dave Coulier. "But I look at them and think, 'I'm so proud of you girls because you've handled it so gracefully.'"

This past year, however, was different. The first public cracks in the foundation appeared just days after their high school graduation in California, when Mary-Kate was treated for an eating disorder, generating almost as much media coverage as the presidential campaign. The 5'2" mega-millionaire spent her landmark 18th birthday (June 13) at a rehab center in Sundance, Utah, before heading to Manhattan in August to enter New York University's Gallatin School of Individualized Study. Mary-Kate appeared to be eating regularly at college and also developed a hearty appetite for the New York nightlife. (Though it wasn't to escape a cramped dorm—the sisters bought a $7.3 million Greenwich Village pad.) The *New York Minute* stars found a second home at Hilton sisters-esque hot spots like Bungalow 8, Butter, Lotus and Marquee, although the underage Olsens were never seen with anything stronger than cigarettes and energy drinks. (Mary-Kate sporadically dated mogul Jeffrey Katzenberg's son David, 21; Ashley broke up with Columbia football player Matt Kaplan, 20.) A weeklong respite in L.A. (where both had voted absentee) sparked rumors that she may quit school, but Mary-Kate returned to class. All the Olsens seem to want at the moment, as Ashley said, is to "live our lives the way we want to live them."

The normally slender Mary-Kate became disturbingly skinny prior to her treatment in June.

BEST USE OF NAKED PULL-UPS

Even among the messy collection of oddballs who dotted the roster of the Boston Red Sox, one player stood out. With his "modern caveman" grooming and laid-back attitude, center fielder **Johnny Damon,** 31, helped further loosen the squad he fondly called a "bunch of idiots" and give Beantown its first World Series crown since 1918. A Kansas-born son of a retired Army sergeant and a Thai native, he quickly won the hearts of Red Sox Nation with his locker-room quirks. "I have this thing I do—I do naked pull-ups," he said. "It's that kind of free style that's propelled us to the next level." Damon's offhand approach landed him a role in Puma's fall ad campaign, which focused on athletes with unconventional personalities. Clearly, there would be no shortage of prospective cave-women, but the divorced father of 5-year-old twins had been engaged since Easter Sunday to Michelle Mangan, a talent agent he met in Houston. "She knew more about cars than I did," said Damon, who gave her a dirt bike for her 29th birthday. Looks like a perfect match.

"It'll stay a little longer," forecasted Damon when asked about the trademark stubble. "Why mess with success?"

"You can't play Ray Charles just as imitation," declared Foxx. "That music has to be in you. You have to know it and feel it."

OUT OF SIGHT, BABY When director Taylor Hackford expressed interest in having him play music legend Ray Charles, **Jamie Foxx**, the TV comedian whose best-known film role at the time was 1997's *Booty Call,* did not play humble. "Jamie's too cool a customer," recalled Hackford. "He just said, 'Yeah, you need me to do it.'" To seal the deal, Foxx, who attended college on a music scholarship, auditioned for Charles in 2002. "It was mind-blowing," said Foxx, 37, who won the blind soul maestro's approval by playing a blues song on piano. "It was spiritual." To prep for each day's shoot, Foxx had his eyelids sealed. "I would get really anxious and feel like I was trapped," he said of the simulated sightlessness. "It was awful, but there's no other way to do it. Ray couldn't just open his eyes between takes. You can't fake it." The payoff was a pitch-perfect performance that left *Ray* reviewers ecstatically predicting an Oscar nomination. "I still have Ray in me," said Foxx, who is single and lives in Los Angeles. "Ray Charles should be in all of us. Anybody can see that, right?"

SHE MADE FAT PHAT

When a guest at her home couldn't choose between a piece of cake or pie for dessert, **Kirstie Alley** suggested he "have both. That's the beauty of being in a fat person's house." In Hollywood, of course, it's taboo to speak of, much less be, plus-size (although the rest of us, doctors say, are becoming dangerously obese). But Alley is disarmingly—and hilariously—candid. "I do not consider fat a disease," said the abundantly overweight 5'8" actress. "I mean, c'mon—who had the f---ing gun to my head? Nobody! What gene in my body says I have to eat four cakes instead of two? It's a choice." Alley, 53, a mother of two who shares custody with ex-husband Parker Stevenson, is so comfortable with her choice that she's starring in *Fat Actress,* a comedy-reality show scheduled for 2005. Each episode is to be based on real-life incidents, like the time a boyfriend saw her naked and, according to her, blurted, "'Wow, you're a big girl.' I weighed 114 lbs., and I looked like friggin' Calista Flockhart!"

"She is a lot like me," said pal John Travolta. "When I gain weight, I enjoy it. She's been very jolly with it." Alley's creed: "Go for the stuff that looks yummy."

ASHLEE SIMPSON

IPODS OF THE STARS!
It may not be a window to the soul, but an iPod playlist displays what's on your mind. We're pretty sure these are the songs that certain celebs couldn't get out of their heads as the year whistled past

JANET JACKSON

MARTHA STEWART

TARA REID

DONALD TRUMP

ASHLEE SIMPSON

It Ain't Me, Babe
Bob Dylan

Voices Carry
'Til Tuesday

The Singer
Not the Song
The Rolling Stones

Girl You Know
It's True
Milli Vanilli

Word Up
Cameo

Found Out About You
Gin Blossoms

HOWARD DEAN

Shout!
The Isley Brothers

Shout It Out Loud
KISS

Scream and Holler
Van Morrison

War ("*What is it good for?*")
Edwin Starr

Bring the Boys
Home
Freda Payne

What'd I Say
Ray Charles

JANET JACKSON

Oops!...I Did It Again
Britney Spears

See Me, Feel Me
The Who

Gettin' Jiggy Wit It
Will Smith

Too Much
Monkey Business
Chuck Berry

Naughty Girl
Beyoncé

Put It Right
Here (Or Keep
It Out There)
Bessie Smith

Milkshake
Kelis

Hey Ya
OutKast

Blame It on
the Tetons
Modest Mouse

MARTHA STEWART

Do You Want to
Know a Secret?
The Beatles

Trouble
Pink

Stupid
Sarah McLachlan

Fallen
Mya

Chain Gang Blues
Ma Rainey

Jailhouse Rock
Elvis Presley

Riot in Cell Block #9
The Robins

I Shall Be Released
Bob Dylan

TARA REID

Let It Out (Let It
All Hang Out)
The Hombres

I Love the Nightlife
Alicia Bridges

Whiskey River
Willie Nelson

Swinging Doors
("*. . . a jukebox and a bar stool*")
Merle Haggard

Hi-Diddle-Dee-Dee
("*It's great to be a celebrity*")
From *Pinocchio*

Tequila
The Champs

Wipe Out
The Surfaris

Never Again, Again
Lee Ann Womack

DONALD TRUMP

Big Boss Man
Jimmy Reed

All Fired Up
Pat Benatar

Call My Job
Detroit Junior

Out of Work
Bruce Springsteen

She's Gone
Hall & Oates

Try a Little
Tenderness
Otis Redding

Money (That's
What I Want)
Barrett Strong

Can't Buy Me Love
The Beatles

Hair
The Cowsills

BILL CLINTON

This Old Heart
of Mine (Is Weak
for You)
The Isley Brothers

Pump It Up
Elvis Costello

Your Cheatin' Heart
Hank Williams

Take My
Breath Away
Jessica Simpson

Numb
Linkin Park

Take These Chains
from My Heart
Ray Charles

Got My Mojo Working
Muddy Waters

BRITNEY SPEARS

White Wedding
Billy Idol

On the Rebound
Uriah Heep

Band of Gold
Freda Payne

Love and Marriage
Frank Sinatra

Private Dancer
Tina Turner

I Was Made to
Love Him
Whitney Houston

Tattooed Love Boys
The Pretenders

Second Hand Rose
Barbra Streisand

Rednecks
Randy Newman

White Trash Beautiful
Everlast

Who'll Be the
Next in Line
The Kinks

Angered by the heavy penalties, Stern called FCC chairman Michael Powell "dangerous to free speech."

TAKE THIS JOB AND . . .

Does **Howard Stern** have a right to be rude?
No #@%& way, said the conservative owners
and overseers of the radio waves. Yanked
from six Clear Channel stations for violating
decency standards in an interview with Paris
Hilton's sex-tape ex, the shock jock also cost
the radio network $1.75 million in FCC fines.
Among other things, he was cited for using
sexual innuendos, which struck fans as the
equivalent of punishing water for evaporating.
In response, Stern announced that he was
leaving free radio and taking his guest strippers,
lesbians and porn stars with him. The King
of All Media set out to conquer another one,
signing a five-year, $500 million deal with
the fledgling SIRIUS Satellite Radio network.
"I know the future," said the 50-year-old
adolescent. "We will be bigger than ever."

"I think he really needs some new suits," a friend said of Clinton, who returned to the campaign trail (and to open his new presidential library in Little Rock) 15 lbs. lighter after surgery.

HEARTIEST STUMPSTER

First he bared all in a blockbuster memoir, writing that he deeply regretted his affair with Monica Lewinsky. "I was misleading everyone about my personal failings," **Bill Clinton** wrote in *My Life,* the hefty 957-page tome that sold more than 2 million copies. "I was embarrassed and wanted to keep it from my wife and daughter, and I didn't want the American people to know I'd let them down. It was like living in a nightmare." The ex-President, who had been kept in the shadows when his veep, Al Gore, lost in 2000, returned to center stage at the Democratic Convention and was poised to lend his charm to the Kerry campaign. But then a life-threatening heart blockage forced him to get quadruple bypass surgery. After recuperating in the upstate New York home he shares with the state's junior senator, the Comeback Kid, 58, returned to the fray during the frantic last week of the race. "Even though my doctor did not prescribe this," he told jubilant supporters, "this is very good for my rehabilitation."

THE DIVA GOES DOWN

Stock fraud? Nonsense. "This is a small personal matter that has been blown out of all proportion," **Martha Stewart** steadfastly maintained, brushing off the accusation like an embarrassing dust bunny in an otherwise impeccably kept life.

In March the domestic diva discovered just how deep a mess she was in, and it was not a good thing. After two years of lurid headlines, Stewart, 63, was found guilty of lying to authorities about her sale of stock in the biotech company ImClone. (Her daughter Alexis, 39, fainted upon hearing the verdict.) Whether she had or hadn't gotten an insider tip from her broker Peter Bacanovic, 42 (also found guilty), the numbers didn't lie: To avoid a relatively measly loss if ImClone shares plummeted, she'd seen her vast fortune fall like a botched soufflé. Gone were $85 million in personal assets and the chairmanship—forever— of the $250 million empire she'd built from scratch in a Connecticut catering kitchen.

Worse, she faced five months in jail—the minimum sentence—as a national lightning rod, pegged by many as yet another corporate criminal getting comeuppance. "This is a victory for the little guys," declared juror Chappell Hartridge, though by any measure Stewart's sins paled next to the lives wrecked by the malfeasance at Enron. "The venom directed toward me has been pretty horrific," she told Barbara Walters. But equally vocal were her many fans and defenders, who saw a powerful woman being punished for doing what they suggested powerful men do every day. They shouted their support from nearby streets in the predawn hours of October 8, when Stewart—determined to be sprung by spring planting season—reported to the minimum-security Alderson Federal Prison Camp (dubbed Camp Cupcake) in bucolic West Virginia. With plans to learn Italian and deals for a post-release book and reality TV show in hand, the heroine of home and hearth was strip-searched and assigned a lower bunk in a densely populated dorm. Yet the message she posted two days later on her Web site— among a deluge of e-mailed encouragement—was typically forthright, practical and upbeat: "The best news—everyone is nice. I have adjusted and am very busy." Martha, being Martha, was multitasking.

"I will be back," Stewart said in a Barbara Walters interview just hours after her sentencing. "I'm used to all kinds of hard work. And I'm not afraid whatsoever."

PUREST POPSTER

"You look so clean, but you spread your dirt/ As if you think your words don't hurt." So sang **Hilary Duff,** the teen princess of all media, in "Haters," from her self-titled sophomore CD. Fans guessed that the 17-year-old Disney Channel deb turned multiplatinum pop and movie star (*A Cinderella Story, Raise Your Voice*) was returning fire in a dissing match with punk-lite rocker Avril Lavigne, 20. Trashed as "a goody-goody" and "mommy's girl," Duff, who lives with her folks and older actor-singer sister Haylie in L.A., held the high road after Lavigne suggested she "shut her mouth." "She's never met Avril," Duff's rep told reporters. "But she is a huge fan of her music."

Duff denied reports of dating Good Charlotte singer Joel Madden, explaining that "we see each other at a lot of events."

BIGGEST MOVIE GAMBLE

Passion plays that dramatize the awful suffering of Christ's last days have been stirring the faithful for centuries. But never has the greatest story been told in such graphic detail and to so loud a ring of cash registers as in **Mel Gibson**'s *The Passion of the Christ.* Hailed as a triumph of Christian belief over Hollywood commercialism, the film drew fans by the flock, pushing the box office to heavenly heights—$600 million and counting—since its Ash Wednesday release. In Hollywood, the film's stunning success was regarded as nothing short of a cinematic miracle. Gibson financed the production almost entirely out of pocket, putting up approximately $30 million when he was unable to find sufficient backers for a film that smart money insisted was a sure flop. A sand-and-sandals epic that graphically depicted the torture, flaying and slaying of Christ was dubious to begin with, the studios reckoned; to film it in the dead language of Aramaic pure folly. In the face of prerelease criticism that the film would ignite a dangerous surge of anti-Semitism, Gibson launched a one-man crusade, screening *The Passion* for evangelical Christian leaders who rallied their followers in support of the film. The strategy, which presaged the Republican wooing of the red-state conservative Christians in the presidential election, easily overcame negative reviews, including one in *The New Yorker* that likened the film's long, excruciating close-ups of Christ's suffering to a "sickening death trip."

While some moviegoers were turned off by Gibson's painful vision, many more were moved to hosannas, with Roger Ebert calling *The Passion* "a very great film." Gibson, 48 and a member of the ultraconservative Traditionalist Catholic movement, has built his own Holy Family Chapel near his Malibu home, where he and his wife, Robyn, and their seven children hear mass in Latin. For him, *The Passion* was personal. When he battled a bout of near-suicidal depression in his mid-30s, Gibson said he found salvation in Jesus' suffering. "I just hit my knees," he said. "And I had to use the Passion of Christ and [his] wounds to heal my wounds."

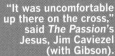

"It was uncomfortable up there on the cross," said *The Passion*'s Jesus, Jim Caviezel (with Gibson).

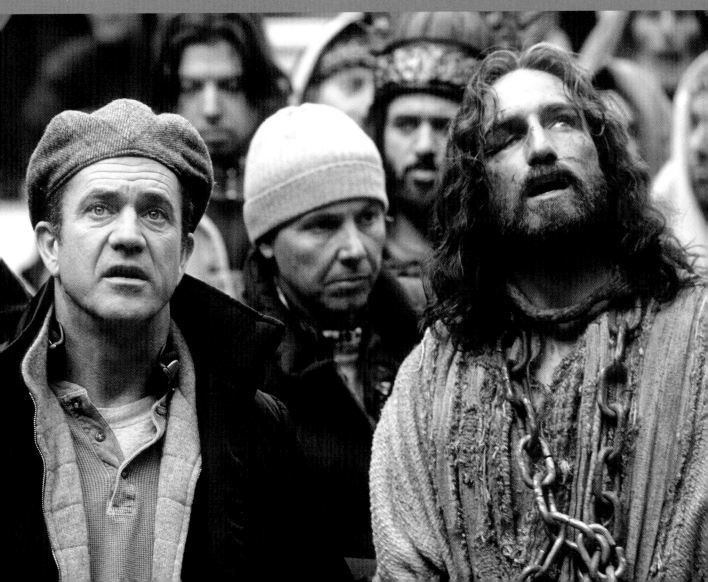

HOTTEST OF THE HOT BUTTONS

As a crusade for equality, proponents equate it to the civil rights movement of the 1950s and 1960s. Opponents view it as an unwanted assault on the family structure as we know it. In the process, the debate over **gay marriage** emerged as one of the most high-decibel issues of a rancorous election season. After simmering for years, the subject caught fire in February when the Massachusetts Supreme Judicial Court ruled it was unconstitutional to deny marriage licenses to same-sex couples.

Within a few days, San Francisco mayor Gavin Newsom was the first of a number of municipal officials to follow the lead. Before being ordered to cease and desist by the California Supreme Court, the city granted 4,161 couples (including Rosie O'Donnell and her partner, Kelli Carpenter) the freedom to tie the knot. "I thought I had an obligation," said Newsom. "I'd just taken an oath as mayor of the most diverse city, where people are living together and prospering together across every conceivable difference."

Once other communities began issuing their own same-sex marriage licenses, the backlash gained force. President Bush lent his support to a proposed federal constitutional amendment banning all same-sex marriages. Senator Kerry, who also opposed gay marriages in favor of slightly more ambiguous civil unions, argued that the decision should be left to the states. On election day, that's exactly what happened. Voters in 11 states dealt a blow to the movement by overwhelmingly approving individual constitutional amendments limiting marriage rites to one man and one woman. End of story? No—gay rights activists are contemplating court challenges against the states. Far from over, the debate has probably just begun.

Minneapolis couple Siddiqi Ray (with bouquet) and partner Liz McElhinney got carried away after their February 15 wedding at San Francisco City Hall.

Jennings's extended run bumped the show's ratings a full 20 percent over the previous year.

LONGEST-RUNNING DWEEB

If **Ken Jennings** is the answer, then the question must be "Who is the top TV game-show winner in history?" The 30-year-old software engineer from Salt Lake City obliterated his competition during an amazing 75-game run on *Jeopardy!,* amassing more than $2.5 million in the process. The beneficiary of a 2003 rule change that removed the show's long-standing five-appearance limit, the straitlaced gadfly rattled off answers like "What is Listerine?" with robotic efficiency. Destined to be known forever as "Jeopardy Guy," the married Mormon (and dad of son Dylan, 2) made the most of his 15 minutes with a victory tour of the talk show circuit, hitting stops like Leno and Letterman before returning to a life filled with much less trivial pursuits.

BEST POP-UP MENU

In the end, it proved to be the money shot seen round the world. Borrowing terminology from the space program to excuse the Super Bowl halftime scandal, Justin Timberlake claimed it was just a "wardrobe malfunction" that caused duet partner **Janet Jackson**'s right breast, decorated with a silver sunburst nipple ring, to jiggle out of her costume before 90 million gawking viewers. While both Jackson and Timberlake apologized and networks vowed to institute delays in future live telecasts, the FCC claimed to have received 540,000 complaints, instigated an investigation and then, seven months after the bare fact, levied a $550,000 fine against the offending broadcaster, CBS. As *Saturday Night Live*'s Jimmy Fallon observed in a Groundhog Day joke, "Janet Jackson's breast popped out of its hole, saw its shadow, and now we'll have six more weeks of overreaction."

This moment was the most TiVo'd in history, noted a spokesman for the instant-replay industry.

WHOOPS!

In a busy year, he was also *SNL* host during the Ashlee Simpson snafu and was narrator of *Lemony Snicket's A Series of Unfortunate Events.*

BEST USE OF AN EMPLOYMENT VISA

If there were an annual prize given to the hardest-working British actor, **Jude Law,** 32, would have won handily in 2004. The gorgeous (and PEOPLE's Sexiest) gent followed up his Oscar nomination for *Cold Mountain* by opening an impressive six films in a year—including Martin Scorsese's *The Aviator* as Errol Flynn. "It's not just how good his work is," said Jon Avnet, producer of his *Sky Captain and the World of Tomorrow,* "it's so much fun with him." One of his costars certainly agreed. Law met current girlfriend Sienna Miller, 23, on the set of the remake of the 1966 comedy *Alfie,* which starred the actor as the womanizing title character.

On the night of her maximum exposure at Diddy's 35th, Paris struck a momentary relatively demure pose.

THE LO-GARB DIET

Shedding threads like so many carbs, marketing natural **Paris Hilton** advanced her campaign to patent the phrase "That's hot," a dialogue tic from her hit reality show *The Simple Life*, by dressing downright feverishly. In her year of high-slit highs and low-cut lows, Hilton, 23, also had a nasty breakup with Backstreet Boy Nick Carter; suffered a nasty break-in at her Hollywood Hills home; lost, then found, her pet pooch Tinkerbell; and savored life as a professional celeb, model, recording artist (her debut album is due in '05) and bestselling author (*Confessions of an Heiress: A Tongue-in-Chic Peek Behind the Pose*). Skimping on clothing through it all, she saved her hottest flash for P. Diddy's infamous birthday bash, topping pal Tara Reid's accidentally exposed breast with a bottom display of her own. There might have been method to her badness; perhaps it was a diversionary tactic. "I desperately hate one thing about my body," she confided in *Confessions*. "I have size-11 feet."

"I think fashion is just in my blood. . . . I started to think seriously about modeling when I was around 15. I was also pretty flat-chested, so what else was I gonna do? Now I'm happy to be small. It looks better in clothes. But back then I was really insecure."
—from *Confessions* (Hilton's, not St. Augustine's)

MAN FROM HOPE II

Referring to America as "a beacon of freedom and opportunity," Illinois state senator **Barack Obama,** 43, transfixed a nationwide audience with his masterful keynote speech at the Democratic National Convention. In a dismal year for Democrats, the Hawaiian-born son of a black Kenyan father and a white woman from Kansas was a singular sensation. Post-convention cachet and unrelenting charisma helped the married father of two win his bid for a U.S. Senate seat by a three-to-one margin; that made him the lone African-American senator and only the third since Reconstruction. So impressive were Obama's "politics of hope" that party leaders began speculating about a future presidential run long before the Harvard Law graduate's first day on Capitol Hill. Despite the trail of expectations behind his rising star, the pol remained focused. "I'm mistrustful of our celebrity culture," he said. "What's lasting is work."

Obama stole the show at the Democratic National Convention in Boston.

SPEEDO FREAK

After his monster performance at the 2004 Summer Olympics, huge hip-hop fan **Michael Phelps** got everything a rapper could desire. In addition to his tricked-out Cadillac Escalade SUV, the superstar swimmer owns a jewelry counter of bling, winning a record-tying eight Olympic medals (six gold, two bronze). The 6'4", 195-lb. swimmer used his size-14 feet, huge hands and lengthy torso to propel himself to six Olympic or world records in Athens. "He's one of the most talented swimmers of all time," said Olympic great Matt Biondi. After the Games, the Maryland native issued a pained public apology for a DUI charge and enrolled at the University of Michigan. A millionaire since turning pro at 16, he planned to train—but can't compete—with the Wolverine swim team.

Only 19, Phelps hopes to inflict further water torture on his opponents at the 2008 Games in China.

THOSE 18 CANDLES REALLY BURNED

Turning 18 is always an event, but in her coming-of-age year, **Lindsay Lohan** proved a poster girl for precocity. The once innocent Disney tween queen starred in Tina Fey's high school satire *Mean Girls,* dealt with her father's repeated arrests (two for assault and one for stiffing a hotel for $3,800), became a player on the gossip pages in the party pack led by Paris Hilton and Nicole Richie, and suffered a 103°-fever attack that sent her to the hospital. Yes, she's *hot.* Along the way, Lohan seemed to be cooking with *That '70s Show's* Wilmer Valderrama, 24, until—oops—they busted up, reportedly because of her uncontrollable flirting. Tough year? Sure, but there's no cause for complaint, according to her mom, Dina, 42. Her advice to her daughter: "I say, 'You're at the top. There's a price for everything. You can't cry and whine. You're a star.'"

"We were all 18 once," philosophized her mother. "All you read about is that she goes out at night, and that's not fair. It's silly—when you're 18, you do go out."

THE UN-GOVERNATOR

"My truth is that I am a gay American." With those words, delivered live on national TV, New Jersey governor **Jim McGreevey,** 47, dropped the political bombshell of the year. His parents and his wife, Dina, to whom he bared his soul just the previous night, were at his side. "If you want me to be there today, I'll be there," she told him shortly before the speech. McGreevey, who won in a landslide in 2001, announced he'd had an affair with a man (a former aide) and that he was resigning effective November. The father of two daughters, one by a previous marriage, publicly apologized to his wife for his "shameful" extramarital affair. "It was wrong," he said. "It was foolish. It was inexcusable." Not long after the speech, Dina bought her own house.

"They were a happy couple," a friend said of McGreevey and Dina. "They were always holding hands, always smiling."

MOST HATED MAN IN THE RED STATES OF AMERICA

The lustiest boos ringing the rafters at Madison Square Garden on the opening night of the Republican National Convention came not at the mention of the Democratic nominee's name but at the sight of an untucked, carbs-loving schlub in a ball cap who happened to be sitting in the press box. **Michael Moore,** 50, the object of the GOP jeering, grinned and flashed the international hand signal for "loser." His possession of media credentials notwithstanding (he was covering the convention for *USA Today*), the muckraking moviemaker said his latest cinematic incendiary device, the antiwar documentary *Fahrenheit 9/11,* was not intended as "a fair and balanced work of journalism." Leave objectivity and non-partisanship to others, added the unabashed Kerry supporter. "I would like to see Mr. Bush removed from the White House."

In past satiric assaults on the establishment, the auteur and provocateur challenged the chairman of Ford to change the oil in an Explorer (*TV Nation*) and filmed a wheelchair-bound shooting victim trying to get a refund from Wal-Mart for the bullets that disabled him (in the Oscar-winning *Bowling for Columbine*). That was the most successful documentary ever—until *9/11* surpassed it with a gross of some $120 million. With its accusations that the President misled the nation into war and caused untold suffering to the Iraqi people, *Fahrenheit* stoked already fiery passions to inferno levels. Conservatives hollered foul, dismissed the film as so much bucks-raking Bush bashing and stopped just short of calling Moore a terrorist—"domestic enemy" was a favored euphemism. Liberals hailed the film for presenting the untold story of the war with footage of baby-faced U.S. soldiers revving up their tank for battle by blasting heavy metal music, Iraqi civilians cowering in their homes and Old Glory-draped coffins shipped home in the dead of night. The Flint, Michigan, native now lives with his wife and daughter in New York City, where he is plotting his next broadsides, *Sicko,* an exposé of the U.S. health-care system, and a sequel to his blockbuster titled *9/11½.*

"Michael's not only funny," said his record-exec friend Danny Goldberg. "He can make you cry."

Pirates of the Caribbean director Gore Verbinski praised Bloom as "beautiful and accessible. As cool as Orlando can be, there is also something there that you can relate to."

DISHIEST DEMIGOD Yeah, yeah, yeah, Brad Pitt in a skirt. Nice, but millions of moviegoers watching the epic *Troy* were grateful, too, that they'd always have Paris—costar **Orlando Bloom** as the impetuous youth who makes off with Helen, sparking the Trojan War. He'd already stolen their hearts—and launched an avalanche of Internet searches—as *The Lord of the Rings'* elf prince Legolas and as Johnny Depp's swashbuckling apprentice in *Pirates of the Caribbean.* But this year the Brit, 27, who dates actress Kate Bosworth, 21, proved he can play with the big boys. Upcoming are a handful of films, including the inevitable *Pirates* sequel, due in 2006. "It's been great to work with Johnny and Brad and pick their brains about how they deal with the fame element," said Bloom, recalling a night out on location in Malta with Pitt. "That was an experience—to see someone get properly mobbed." Best get used to it.

Hung (performing a rendition of "She Bangs" at a UC Berkeley volleyball game) doesn't drink, smoke or swear, though he has confessed to sometimes using the phrase "What the heck is going on here?"

BAD TO THE BONE "You can't sing [and] you can't dance." And with that seemingly fatal pronouncement by *American Idol* judge Simon Cowell after a truly awful butchering of Ricky Martin's "She Bangs" by **William Hung,** a star was born. A Hong Kong-born UC Berkeley civil engineering student, Hung, 22, accepted defeat and insults about everything from his looks to his naïveté so gracefully that he prevailed, scoring his own hit LP *Inspiration,* which sold an astonishing 380,000 copies. He promoted it on the networks and then hit the road for Hong Kong and Singapore to push his follow-up, a nicely titled EP of Christmas songs—*Hung for the Holidays.* "Okay, so I'm not famous for the right reasons," he said with typically disarming Popeye-like honesty. "I'm infamous, a joke . . . but I don't let it get to me because I am who I am."

ROCK THE QUOTE

From the mouths of babes—and dudes, too—came an unforgettable earful of bons mots, put-downs, rants and loose thoughts

> Someone called me and said, "You're on the *New York Times* bestsellers list," and I was like, "Is that good?"
>
> **PAMELA ANDERSON,** on her book *Star*

The camp is like an old-fashioned college campus—without the freedom, of course.
MARTHA STEWART, in a posting on her Web site, about life at the Alderson Federal Prison Camp

It's crazy. Do you realize we landed on Mars that day? Why aren't we all talking about that?
BRITNEY SPEARS, on the attention her 55-hour first marriage received

[Kabbalah] helps you confront your fears. Like if a girl borrowed my clothes and never gave them back and I saw her wearing them months later, I would confront her.
PARIS HILTON

I've never been to rehab. I've never been to jail. Never been arrested. All the child-star clichés.
MACAULAY CULKIN, now 24, three months before his bust for pot possession

Obviously, it's not nice to shoot people.
Former Long Island Lolita AMY FISHER, discussing her crime on *Oprah*

Apples are so sweet and they're wholesome.... Then she was born, and it became an international outrage.
GWYNETH PALTROW, on naming her baby Apple

Jennifer Lopez was married over the weekend. And she married salsa heartthrob Marc Anthony. No date has been set for the divorce.
DAVID LETTERMAN

In Hollywood, I see many starving people every day. We call them actresses. Ironically, when offered food, they decline.
***Will & Grace*'s SEAN HAYES**

If I can sell tickets to my movies like *Red Sonja* or *Last Action Hero,* you know I can sell just about anything.
GOV. ARNOLD SCHWARZENEGGER, promising to lure more jobs to California

I know a great deal about the Middle East because I've been raising Arabian horses for over 20 years; I've researched the culture for most of my life.
PATRICK SWAYZE, discussing the Iraq war

Cartoon character Cathy finally got engaged to her boyfriend in today's Valentine edition of her strip. Meanwhile, Marcie and Peppermint Patty are moving to Massachusetts.
TINA FEY on *Saturday Night Live*

> It's the sort of vague calm you get after vomiting—where the vomit itself is rather unpleasant, but when it's over it does bring you a kind of strange peace
>
> **BEN AFFLECK, on being out of the Bennifer spotlight**

Being shot in the face, I lost a tooth. Gums too. And my voice changed. There's a little hiss. [Now] this is the voice that sells millions of records
50 CENT

Pick up your s---
MADONNA, revealing her mothering mantra on *20/20*

I wouldn't kick President Bush out of my bed. Although I do think he needs some sassy highlights.
Queer Eye's **CARSON KRESSLEY**

I could argue with this spoon, and it would be the same as arguing with you.
NICK LACHEY to Jessica Simpson on *Newlyweds*

It was very uncomfortable up there on the cross.
JIM CAVIEZEL, on starring in Mel Gibson's *Passion*

Life is not worth living unless there is a camera around.
CARMEN ELECTRA

I guess it's a sign that I'm moving up the ladder: The gay rumors are starting.
HUGH JACKMAN

Rude, vile pigs.
SIR ELTON JOHN, on a paparazzi pack

I'm not ready to be at home with a baby.
PENELOPE CRUZ

Your dirty laundry gets out of school at 2:30 every day. They can't read, they can't write . . . they're going nowhere.
BILL COSBY, in a critique of some African-American parents

She was conscious of her breasts, so I bought her a new pair. I liked them for a while, but if I had the chance again, I'd buy her a car.
USHER, on getting implants for an ex-girlfriend

It means sexy boys throw themselves at me. And I can borrow lots of designer dresses.
SCARLETT JOHANSSON, on the rush of fame in the wake of *Lost in Translation*

DECISIVE MOMENTS

From sensational criminal cases and devastating storms at home
to horrific terror attacks and a climbing death toll abroad,
these were key events that shaped the year and shook our world

Belying their happy-couple portrait, Peterson, said prosecutors, planned Laci's murder in order to escape his responsibilities as a husband and dad-to-be. "I was hoping for infertility" was his answer when asked if he was looking forward to fatherhood.

A GUILTY VERDICT IN LACI'S MURDER

From the start, it looked like Scott Peterson might be able to pull an O.J. There were no eyewitnesses and a paucity of physical evidence connecting the suave, confident and photogenic Peterson, now 32, to the crime of murdering his wife, Laci, 27. She was eight months pregnant with the couple's first child when her decomposed body was found along the shore of San Francisco Bay, and prosecutors presented a case as flimsy in parts as, literally, a meringue.

In his opening arguments, lead prosecutor Rick Distaso ridiculed Peterson's statements to police, among them that he and Laci had watched Martha Stewart whip up meringue on TV in their Modesto, California, home the morning of December 24, 2002—the day he

THE AMBER PHONE TRANSCRIPT

JAN. 6, 2003 SCOTT: I lied to you that I've been traveling. . . . The girl I'm married to, her name is Laci. . . . She disappeared before Christmas.
AMBER: You came to me in early December and told me you lost your wife. What

was that about?
S: She's alive. . . . The media has been telling everyone that I had something to do with her disappearance. . . . I hope so much that this doesn't hurt you. . . . You deserve so much better.
A: Yeah, and I deserve . . . an explanation of why you told me you lost your wife and this was the first holidays you'd

spend without her. This was December 9th. . . . You sat there in front of me and cried and broke down. I sat there and held your hand, Scott, and comforted you, and you have lied to me.
S: Yeah.
A: Didn't you say, "Amber, I will do anything for you to trust me. . . . I feel we have a future together."

S: I never said anything to you that I didn't mean.
JAN. 7 A: Scott, you really haven't done everything you can yet [to find Laci]. You don't speak in public. . . . You have nothing to hide?
S: No. . . . Everyone's the suspect. I'm the prime suspect.
A: And you haven't [gone] before the media . . . to plead innocent in any of this?

reported her missing. In fact, stated Distaso, the episode had aired the day before, implying that even in so seemingly insignificant a detail Peterson couldn't keep his story straight. The salvo backfired, however, when Peterson's high-profile attorney Mark Geragos proved that the episode, meringue and all, did indeed air on the 24th. It was the first of many holes that the defense shot in the prosecution's case, which was further wounded by Distaso's numbing courtroom style and a series of procedural blunders that led the judge to chew out the prosecutors in front of the jury on three separate occasions. What a state attorney had once termed a "slam dunk" case against a defendant the world believed was guilty, appeared, after five months of testimony, dead in the water.

Enter Amber Frey. A single mother, Frey, 29, had met Peterson at the World Sports Cafe in Fresno and begun an affair with him in November 2002. It took Frey just a week of riveting testimony to single-handedly salvage the prosecution case. In a soft, girlish voice, she described how Peterson, a serial adulterer who had had at least two other affairs during his five-year marriage to Laci, seduced her with hints of marriage and informed her, three weeks before Laci's disappearance, that his wife was dead. Momentum swung even more dramatically toward the prosecution after hours of Peterson's taped phone conversations with Frey were played in open court. The police, who had suspected Peterson all along, had tapped his calls. At one point, the courtroom erupted in scornful laughter when Frey, who had also begun to suspect her lover was guilty, asked him what Laci's response had been when he supposedly told her he was seeing Amber. "Fine," Peterson said. "Fine?"

Laci's supporters created a shrine in Modesto, with a replica of the boat Peterson claimed he took out fishing the day she went missing. Prosecutors say Peterson (above, with Geragos, left) transported Laci's body in the boat, after murdering her in their home.

responded Frey. "A [pregnant] woman, fine about another woman?" The tapes, said legal experts, were devastating to the defense case, which seemed to unravel thereafter. Once jury deliberations began in November 2004, however, all bets were off. "One holdout," said an observer, "could have caused a hung jury." That prospect seemed likely when three members of the jury had to be replaced. Thus the verdict, when it came, was met by stunned cheers outside the courtroom. "We got him!" Laci's father was heard shouting into his cell phone later. "We got the guilty son of a bitch! It's a very good day."

S: I am innocent. I don't have to plead it.
A: [I have] this fear inside my heart that you had something to do with this and that you may have . . . killed your wife.
S: No, you don't need to have that fear. I lied to you. But I'm not an evil person.
A: What are you willing to do for me so that I can trust you and believe and know in my

heart that . . . you had nothing to do with her [disappearance]?
S: Anything you ask. . . . After we find Laci, anything you ask is done.
JAN. 8 A: If Laci already knows about me . . . why did you keep up [the] deception?
S: Just so I wouldn't, you know, hurt other people.
A: You didn't only lie to me, you've lied to a nation, Scott.

S: No, I haven't.
A: One, you have not spoke in public . . . a husband of a missing pregnant woman. . . . So, did you love Laci and your baby?
S: I love Laci. I loved Laci, no question.
A: So you loved her, but there's me. How does that make sense? How . . . how can I make sense of that, Scott?

THE IRAQI HORROR PICTURE SHOW

When *The New Yorker* published the devastating photos of prisoner abuse at Abu Ghraib prison near Baghdad, cries of outrage resounded around the world. "The rules for the treatment of prisoners of war are very clear," said Senator John McCain, a POW himself for 5½ years in North Vietnam. "There is no justification for this kind of treatment." Top brass at the Pentagon quickly blamed the violations on a few bad apples in the 372nd Military Police Company. The most infamous were Spc. Charles Graner, 36, and his pregnant fiancée, Pfc. Lynndie England, 21; five other key participants also faced criminal charges in the physical torture and sexual humiliation documented on-camera.

Despite appearing quite jovial in the assorted shots, England, who gave birth to a baby boy later in the year, claimed to be an unwilling participant in the prisoner mistreatment. The Fort Ashby, West Virginia, native insisted that her superiors at the prison—"Everyone in the company from the commander down"—were aware of what was happening and condoned it. Brig. Gen. Janis Karpinski, who oversaw the prison and was suspended from her duties, intimated that Defense Department officials had implicitly approved aggressive methods to get suspects to talk.

The prison itself had ironically earned a brutal reputation as one of Saddam Hussein's most notorious locales for committing mass executions and inflicting horrible torture upon his Iraqi opponents. Despite cries for the demolition of Abu Ghraib, the building will remain standing through the participants' trials, since it was declared a crime scene by military judge Col. James Pohl. The seven court-martialed soldiers were all reservists, and their family and friends attributed their actions to inexperience and inadequate instruction in prisoner control. "My son is not a trained MP," said Daniel Sivits, whose son, Spc. Jeremy Sivits, 25, pleaded guilty to his role in the scandal. "He is trained as a mechanic. . . . He's used to changing tires on a Humvee." First Lt. David Sutton, 38, who blew the whistle on some of the abuse at Abu Ghraib, disagreed. "It's not rocket science," he said. "It's basic how you treat human beings—you don't do certain things."

A prisoner was costumed and told he would be electrocuted if he stepped off the box (top). England held a nude captive by a leash (bottom).

The tab for taxpayers: $400,000 to cover the costs of 44 filings, 800 pleadings and 999 jury summonses.

KOBE BRYANT'S FIRST TRIAL ENDS

Fourteen months after accusing Los Angeles Laker Kobe Bryant of sexually assaulting her in an Edwards, Colorado, hotel room, his alleged victim called prosecutors during jury selection and told them she had decided not to testify. "It was a horrible daily struggle for her," said Dana Easter, one of the lead prosecutors. The withdrawal of the now 20-year-old prime witness brought an abrupt finale to an ordeal that had taken a heavy toll on both accuser and accused. Throughout the pretrial, the accuser had been portrayed by the defense team and in lurid media reports as a starstruck girl with questionable mental health and a promiscuous sex life. Bryant, who claimed the encounter was consensual, issued a statement apologizing for his "behavior that night." Thanks in part to a $4 million ring he gave his wife, Vanessa, 22, his marriage still seemed intact. But his cred as one of the NBA's major role models was in jeopardy— McDonald's, among other companies, dropped the 26-year-old all-star as a spokesman. Nor were his legal troubles over. The accuser filed a civil suit but because of Colorado's strict limits on financial penalties was considering refiling in Bryant's home state of California, seeking unspecified damages for pain and suffering.

After special forces entered the besieged school, soldiers helped evacuate young hostages amid continued shooting and explosions.

A LOSS OF INNOCENTS IN RUSSIA

For children the world over, the first day of school is occasion for excitement and anticipation. But for the pupils, teachers and parents at School No. 1 in Beslan, Russia, the day turned into one of almost unimaginable horror. "It was a bright sunny morning," recalled one mother, who had stopped with her 12-year-old daughter to buy flowers for the teacher. Then, as the kids were lining up in the playground, she reported seeing "a man running at us with a machine gun." So began a 62-hour siege in which 32 masked and heavily armed terrorists from the dissident province of Chechnya herded more than 1,000 helpless hostages into a stifling gymnasium, booby-trapped it with bombs and stunned the world, which viewed the ensuing tragedy on TV. "Russian soldiers are killing our children in Chechnya," a terrorist told a physics teacher, "so we are here to kill yours." The standoff ended when a bomb that had been taped to a basketball hoop fell, setting off an explosion. The ceiling of the gym collapsed, and a gun battle began. When it finally ended, 335 hostages, nearly half of them children, had died and hundreds more were wounded. For survivors, the trauma lingers. "Last night she woke up and started shouting for water, like she was dying of thirst," a mother said of her 7-year-old daughter. "She was having a nightmare from those days in the gym."

MISSING
FROM CITY CREEK CANYON OR MEMORY GROVE AREA

LORI HACKING
27 YEARS OLD 5'4" 100 LBS
PLEASE CONTACT POLICE: 799-3000
WITH ANY INFORMATION

Signs went up in Salt Lake City right after Lori's disappearance. Though her family hoped Mark would admit the crime in court, he pleaded not guilty to murder.

CAUGHT IN A WEB OF LIES

Everything seemed perfect. Happily married to his high school sweetheart, Lori, Mark Hacking was about to take the first step toward his lifelong dream of becoming a doctor like his father. As he prepared to move from Salt Lake City to North Carolina to begin medical school, Lori, who helped pay for his schooling by working in a bank, had just learned that she was pregnant with their first child. So friends and family were shocked when Mark raised the alarm that Lori, 27, had disappeared while jogging in a city park, and hundreds joined the search for the hardworking mom-to-be. Then it got weird. In a routine background check of the missing woman's husband, police began to turn up a disturbing chain of deceptions. Mark, 28, had not been accepted nor even applied to med school in North Carolina. He had secretly dropped out of college in '02 but continued to pretend to be a student. "He'd study, do his homework, write papers," recalled a colleague at a psychiatric hospital where Mark worked. Then police found a blood-stained knife with strands of hair in the couple's apartment. Mark was hospitalized after he was discovered naked and disoriented in a hotel parking lot the night after Lori's disappearance. Less than a week later, Mark allegedly confessed to his brothers that he had shot Lori in the head as she slept and thrown her body into a Dumpster. After a painful two-month wait, her remains were found in a landfill; Mark was charged with first-degree murder. "Our lives will never be the same," said Lori's mother, who looked forward to being a grandmother. "We will grieve for her and miss her until the day we die."

TRUE CRIME THRILLER

Here's one government report they won't be recommending at sleep clinics. TIME called *The 9/11 Commission Report* "one of the most riveting, disturbing and revealing accounts of crime, espionage and the inner workings of government ever written." The unlikely page-turner (567 of them) topped the *New York Times* bestseller list for 11 weeks and sold more than 1.5 million copies. Literary luminary John Updike likened the report prepared by the 10 commissioners and 81 staffers to "our language's lone masterpiece produced by committee"—the King James Bible.

"What makes me so special?" Tillman asked his agent Frank Bauer after turning down a seven-figure movie and book offer.

A MAN OF HONOR

At a time when the word "hero" is carelessly tossed around, Pat Tillman was the genuine article. Walking away from a $3.6 million contract and NFL stardom to enlist in the Army Rangers post-9/11, the defensive back sacrificed even more when he was killed by friendly fire while keeping the peace in Afghanistan. It was his second posting there, with a tour in Iraq in between. "While many of us will be blessed to live a longer life," said Arizona senator John McCain, "few of us will ever lead a better one." Tillman, 27, and his brother Kevin, 26, who enlisted together, resisted any publicity because they didn't want to upstage their fellow servicemen. A specialist at the end, he was promoted posthumously to corporal and awarded the Silver Star. In addition to Kevin, Tillman left behind his wife of almost two years, high school sweetheart Marie, 28. Said quarterback Jake Plummer, his teammate at Arizona State and with the NFL Cardinals: "He was one of a kind."

HURRICANE DEVASTATION

They may sound like names of friends, but Charley, Frances, Ivan and Jeanne—the consecutive hurricanes that wreaked deadly havoc on the southeastern U.S. during August and September—bring anything but fond memories. Florida, the hardest hit of all the states, was socked with $42 billion in storm-related damage. The human suffering was beyond measure as millions endured lengthy power outages, thousands lost homes and more than 80 people died. "Everything's gone—everything," said Doug Pacitti, 31, whose rented Pensacola home was demolished during Hurricane Ivan. "Three thousand dollars worth of fishing poles. The antique dishes my grandmother gave me—gone. Even my kid's toys." For all its misery, the worst hurricane season in 118 years did manage to showcase the best elements of the human spirit. Take Jim Williams, a Sanford letter carrier. "I sat in my truck and cried," he recalled of his drive to work in the aftermath of Hurricane Charley. Then, every day for the next three weeks, Williams, 45, devoted hours after his shift to chainsawing and clearing debris from the homes of the many retirees along his 18-mile mail route. "I did what I could to help," said Williams, who refused payment but did accept one token of gratitude: a pecan pie.

A marina in Fort Pierce City, Florida, in the wake of Hurricane Frances.

ELIZABETH EDWARDS'S BATTLE

After enduring an emotionally draining challenge that few experience, Elizabeth Edwards confronted another that is sadly familiar to too many. Hours after she watched her husband, John, concede defeat in his race to become Vice President, Edwards learned that the next fight she had to face—against breast cancer—was one she had to win. A week later she began chemotherapy to reduce a half-dollar-size lump she discovered in her right breast during the closing days of the campaign. After the projected 16-week treatment, she expected to have the lump surgically removed. Edwards, 55, a lawyer and the mother of three (ages 22, 6 and 4), was the latest in a series of prominent women diagnosed with the disease. Earlier, *Sopranos* star Edie Falco successfully completed a course of therapy and Grammy-winning rocker Melissa Etheridge underwent surgery to remove a tumor and surrounding lymph nodes. While all three women expressed confidence that they acted in time, there was a measure of uncertainty as well as hope. Two days before the election, and on the last day of Breast Cancer Awareness Month, a cancer patient handed Edwards one of the pink ribbons symbolizing the battle against the disease, which were almost as ubiquitous as campaign buttons. The woman asked, "'Are you a breast cancer survivor?'" Edwards recalled. "And I thought to myself: I don't know the answer to that."

"In a sense, having cancer takes you by the shoulders and shakes you," Edwards said, chastizing herself for not having a mammogram since the birth in 2000 of her youngest child.

A rescuer said he'd always remember "all the people asking for help that I couldn't help—because they were going to die anyway."

TERROR ON THE TRACKS

With the sinister precision of the September 11 terror attacks, the bombs were timed to inflict maximum carnage among as many defenseless people as possible in Spain's capital. The killing machinery was as ordinary as the victims' morning commute by rail from their suburban homes to their workplaces and schools in Madrid. Ten bombs, each made by packing a cell phone and dozens of nails and screws into a large tote bag along with detonator wires and 22 pounds of a gelatinous form of dynamite, were exploded in four commuter trains at the height of the morning rush hour just three days before the Spanish election. The coordinated attack—bombs were triggered by a preset cell phone alarm—killed more than 200 and wounded upwards of 1,500 more. "You love life," an al-Qaeda operative said in a tape claiming credit for the carnage, "and we love death." The explosion led to a change of government in Spain, where many voters, already opposing the prime minister's support of the U.S.-led war on Iraq, regarded his original (and false) blame of Basque separatists for the terrorist attack as the final straw. It was felt in Washington as well when the new administration in Madrid withdrew Spanish troops from the coalition forces in Iraq. Politics aside, the bombing would be etched forever in the memories of many shattered families. "I don't know why it happened," said a 10-year-old émigré from Morocco. "The terrorists don't win anything. There are people dying, people suffering. I hope the terrorists will know how people feel after the attack."

THE GREATEST SACRIFICE

As the number of servicemen and -women who have died in Iraq passed 1,200, America mourned their loss along with their families, friends and fellow citizens. Here's the sad roll call

The pacifist American Friends Service Committee assembled this poignant memorial in Indianapolis on September 11, 2004.

Spec. Jeremy L. Ridlen
23
IL

Joseph Camara
Michael C. Campbell
Ryan M. Campbell
Marvin A. Camposiles
Isaac Campoy
Wesley J. Canning
Jakia S. Cannon
Ervin Caradine Jr.
Adolfo C. Carballo
Michael M. Carey
Richard P. Carl
Ryan G. Carlock
Benjamin R. Carman
Edward W. Carman
Jocelyn L. Carrasquillo
David M. Caruso
Frank T. Carvill
Jose Casanova
Christopher S. Cash
Ahmed A. Cason
James A. Casper
Paul J. Cassidy
Roland L. Castro
Sean K. Cataudella
Steven C. T. Cates
Thomas D. Caughman
James W. Cawley
Jessica L. Cawvey
David A. Cedergren
Manuel A. Ceniceros
Doron Chan
Kemaphoom A. Chanawongse
James A. Chance III
William D. Chaney
Robert William Channell Jr.
Jason K. Chappell
Jonathan M. Cheatham
Yihjyh L. Chen
Marcus M. Cherry
Therrel S. Childers
Andrew F. Chris
Thomas W. Christensen
Brett T. Christian
Arron R. Clark
Michael J. Clark
Don A. Clary
Donald J. Cline Jr.
Christopher R. Cobb
Kyle W. Codner
Christopher D. Coffin
Bradli N. Coleman
Gary B. Coleman
Benjamin J. Colgan
Russell L. Collier
Gary L. Collins
Jonathan W. Collins
Lawrence S. Colton
Zeferino E. Colunga
Robert E. Colvill Jr.
Kenneth Conde Jr.
Timothy M. Conneway
Steven D. Conover
Aaron J. Contreras
Pedro Contreras
Jason Cook
Eric F. Cooke
Todd R. Cornell
Dennis A. Corral
Alexander S. Coulter
Kelley L. Courtney
Leonard M. Cowherd
Gregory A. Cox
Ryan R. Cox
Timothy R. Creager
Michael T. Crockett
Ricky L. Crockett
Brud J. Cronkrite
Kyle D. Crowley
Rey D. Cuervo
Kevin A. Cuming
Daniel Francis J. Cunningham
Darren J. Cunningham
Carl F. Curran
Michael Edward Curtin
Christopher E. Cutchall
Brian K. Cutter
Edgar P. Daclan Jr.
Anthony D. D'Agostino
Nathan S. Dalley
Andrew S. Dang
Danny B. Daniels II
Torey J. Dantzler
Norman Darling
Eric B. Das
Shawn M. Davies
Brandon L. Davis
Craig Davis
Donald N. Davis
Raphael S. Davis
Wilbert Davis
Jeffrey F. Dayton
Jason L. Deibler
Lauro G. DeLeon Jr.
Felix M. Delgreco
Jacob H. Demand
Kevin J. Dempsey
Mike A. Dennie
Darryl T. Dent
Ervin Dervishi
Daniel A. Desens
Travis R. Desiato
Michael R. Deuel
Michael J. Deutsch
Christopher M. Dickerson
Nicholas J. Dieruf

Jeremiah J. DiGiovanni
Catalin D. Dima
Jeremy M. Dimaranan
Michael A. Diraimondo
Anthony J. Dixon
Thomas K. Doerflinger
Ryan E. Doltz
Michael E. Dooley
Patrick D. Dorff
Trace W. Dossett
Scott E. Dougherty
Robert J. Dowdy
Stephen P. Downing II
Chad H. Drake
Jeremy L. Drexler
Christopher M. Duffy
Jason L. Dunham
Joe L. Dunigan Jr.
Robert L. DuSang
William D. Dusenbery
Seth J. Dvorin
Jason B. Dwelley
Richard S. Eaton Jr.
Christopher S. Ebert
William C. Eckhart
Marshall L. Edgerton
Shawn C. Edwards
Andrew C. Ehrlich
Aaron C. Elandt
Justin M. Ellsworth
William R. Emanuel IV
Mark E. Engel
Peter G. Enos
Pedro I. Espaillat Jr.
Adam W. Estep
Ruben Estrella-Soto
David Evans Jr.
Mark A. Evnin
Jeremy Ricardo Ewing
Justin L. Eyerly
Jonathan I. Falaniko
Steven W. Faulkenburg
James D. Faulkner
Raymond J. Faulstich Jr.
Brian R. Faunce
Arthur L. Felder
Tyanna S. Felder
Paul M. Felsberg
Rian C. Ferguson
Richard L. Ferguson
George A. Fernandez
Clint D. Ferrin
Jon P. Fettig
Tyler R. Fey
Luis A. Figueroa
Jeremy J. Fischer
Paul F. Fisher
Dustin R. Fitzgerald
Jacob S. Fletcher
Francisco A. Martinez Flores
Ricardo Flores-Mejia
Thomas A. Foley III
Timothy Folmar
Elia P. Fontecchio
Jason C. Ford
Travis A. Ford
Wesley C. Fortenberry
Maurice Keith Fortune
Bradley C. Fox
Travis A. Fox
Craig S. Frank
Phillip E. Frank
Bobby C. Franklin
Robert L. Frantz
Benjamin L. Freeman
Bryan L. Freeman
David K. Fribley
David T. Friedrich
Luke P. Frist
Adam D. Froehlich
Kurt R. Frosheiser
Nichole M. Frye
Kane M. Funke
Dan H. Gabrielson
Jonathan E. Gadsden
Richard J. Gannon II
Tomas Garces
Derek L. Gardner
Jose A. Garibay
Joseph M. Garmback Jr.
Landis W. Garrison
Justin W. Garvey
Joseph P. Garyantes
Israel Garza
Joe J. Garza
Juan Guadalupe Garza Jr.
Dimitrios Gavriel
Christopher D. Gelineau
Cory Ryan Geurin
Peter J. Giannopoulos
Christopher A. Gibson
Jonathan L. Gifford
Kyle C. Gilbert
Cornell W. Gilmore
Ronald A. Ginther
Jesse A. Givens
Michael T. Gleason
Todd J. Godwin
James Michael Goins
Christopher A. Golby
David J. Goldberg
Shane L. Goldman
Armando Ariel Gonzalez
Benjamin R. Gonzalez
Jesus A. Gonzalez
Jorge A. Gonzalez
Victor A. Gonzalez

Roberto Abad
Michael D. Acklin II
Genaro Acosta
Steven Acosta
James F. Adamouski
Algernon Adams
Brandon E. Adams
Clarence Adams III
Michael R. Adams
Michael S. Adams
Thomas Mullen Adams
Jamaal R. Addison
Patrick R. Adle
Jeramy A. Ailes
Tristan N. Aitken
Segun Frederick Akintade
Nickalous N. Aldrich
Ronald D. Allen Jr.
Glenn R. Allison
Michael J. Allred
Eric L. Allton
Nicanor Alvarez
John D. Amos II
Brian E. Anderson
Carl L. Anderson Jr.
Michael C. Anderson
Nathan R. Anderson
Nicholas H. Anderson
Michael Andrade
Joe M. Aneiros
Levi T. Angell
Edward J. Anguiano
Andrew Todd Arnold
Alexander S. Arredondo

Jimmy J. Arroyave
Robert R. Arsiaga
Evan Asa Ashcraft
Shawn M. Atkins
Jay Thomas Aubin
Steven E. Auchman
Matthew J. August
Aaron C. Austin
Andrew Julian Aviles
Eric A. Ayon
Travis S. Babbitt
Henry A. Bacon
Andrew Joseph Baddick
Daniel A. Bader
Nathan J. Bailey
Brian K. Baker
Ronald W. Baker
Ryan T. Baker
Sherwood R. Baker
Chad E. Bales
Kenneth Michael Ballard
Solomon C. Bangayan
Juan C. Cabral Banuelos
Dominic R. Baragona
Mark A. Barbret
Collier E. Barcus
Michael C. Barkey
Jonathan P. Barnes
Edward C. Barnhill
Jeremiah A. Baro
Aric J. Barr
Michael Paul Barrera
Douglas E. Bascom
Todd M. Bates
Michael Battles Sr.

Jorge A. Molina Bautista
Alan N. Bean Jr.
Bradley S. Beard
Beau R. Beaulieu
Ryan Anthony Beaupre
James L. Beckstrand
Mick R. Bekowsky
Gregory A. Belanger
Christopher Belchik
Aubrey D. Bell
Wilfred D. Bellard
Joseph P. Bellavia
William M. Bennett
Robert T. Benson
David R. Bernstein
Joel L. Bertoldie
Stephen A. Bertolino Sr.
Marvin Best
Mark A. Bibby
Benjamin W. Biskie
Michael E. Bitz
Jarrod W. Black
Thomas A. Blair
Michael T. Blaise
Ernesto A. Blanco
James D. Blankenbecler
James P. Blecksmith
Joseph M. Blickenstaff
Nicholas H. Blodgett
Trevor A. Blumberg
Jeremy L. Bohlman
Jeffrey E. Bohr Jr.
Todd J. Bolding
Dennis J. Boles
Craig A. Boling

Kelly Bolor
Stevon A. Booker
Clarence E. Boone
John J. Boria
Rachel K. Bosveld
Mathew G. Boule
Elvis Bourdon
Jeremy D. Bow
Samuel R. Bowen
Theodore A. Bowling
Hesley Box Jr.
Noah L. Boye
Aaron Boyles
Edward W. Brabazon
Travis J. Bradach-Nall
Kenneth R. Bradley
Stacey C. Brandon
David M. Branning
Artimus D. Brassfield
Joel K. Brattain
Jeffrey F. Braun
William I. Brennan
Steven H. Bridges
Kyle A. Brinlee
Cory W. Brooks
Thomas F. Broomhead
Andrew W. Brown
Bruce E. Brown
Dominic C. Brown
Henry L. Brown
John E. Brown
Larry K. Brown
Lunsford B. Brown II
Nathan P. Brown
Philip D. Brown

Tyler H. Brown
Andrew D. Brownfield
Nathan B. Bruckenthal
Cedric E. Bruns
Benjamin S. Bryan
Todd J. Bryant
Ernest G. Bucklew
Roy Russell Buckley
Paul J. Bueche
Charles H. Buehring
Brian Rory Buesing
George Edward Buggs
Joshua I. Bunch
Christopher Bunda
Michael L. Burbank
Richard A. Burdick
Dale A. Burger Jr.
Alan J. Burgess
Jeffrey C. Burgess
Tamario D. Burkett
Travis L. Burkhardt
Kyle W. Burns
David P. Burridge
Jesse R. Buryj
Charles E. Bush Jr.
Matthew D. Bush
Damian S. Bushart
Jacob L. Butler
Joshua T. Byers
John T. Byrd II
Marshall H. Caddy
Cody S. Calavan
Juan Calderon Jr.
Charles T. Caldwell
Nathaniel A. Caldwell

Bernard G. Gooden
Gregory R. Goodrich
Richard S. Gottfried
Richard A. Goward
Jeffrey C. Graham
Jamie A. Gray
Michael J. Gray
Tommy L. Gray
Torrey L. Gray
Jeffrey G. Green
David S. Greene
Devin J. Grella
Kyle A. Griffin
Patrick Lee Griffin Jr.
Sean R. Grilley
Joseph R. Guerrera
Hans N. Gukeisen
Christian D. Gurtner
Analaura Esparza Gutierrez
Jose Gutierrez
Richard W. Hafer
Guy S. Hagy Jr.
Charles G. Haight
Michael J. Halal
Deryk L. Hallal
Jesse M. Halling
Andrew Halverson
Erik A. Halvorsen
Nathaniel T. Hammond
Kimberly N. Hampton
Michael S. Hancock
Michael W. Hanks
Fernando B. Hannon
Warren S. Hansen
James W. Harlan
Atanasio Haro-Marin
William M. Harrell
Foster L. Harrington
Adam J. Harris
Kenneth W. Harris Jr.
Torry D. Harris
Leroy Harris-Kelly
John D. Hart
Nathaniel Hart Jr.
David A. Hartman
Jonathan N. Hartman
Stephen C. Hattamer
Sheldon R. Hawk Eagle
Omer T. Hawkins II
Timothy L. Hayslett
Brian D. Hazelgrove
David M. Heath
Justin W. Hebert
Christopher T. Heflin
Damian L. Heidelberg
Raheen Tyson Heighter
Jeremy M. Heines
Brian R. Hellerman
Terry W. Hemingway
Matthew C. Henderson
Robert L. Henderson II
Kenneth W. Hendrickson
Jack T. Hennessy
Joshua J. Henry
Clayton W. Henson
Armando Hernandez
Joseph F. Herndon II
Edward J. Herrgott
Jacob R. Herring
Gregory B. Hicks
Christopher K. Hill
Stephen D. Hiller
Keicia M. Hines
Melissa J. Hobart
Erick J. Hodges
Nicholas M. Hodson
James T. Hoffman
Theodore S. Holder II
Christopher J. Holland
Fern L. Holland
Aaron N. Holleyman
Lincoln D. Hollinsaid
James J. Holmes
Jeremiah J. Holmes
Terry Holmes
Antoine J. Holt
Sean Horn
Kelly L. Hornbeck
Jeremy R. Horton
Andrew R. Houghton
John R. Howard
Gregory C. Howman
Bert E. Hoyer
Jared P. Hubbard
Tavon L. Hubbard
Corey A. Hubbell
Christopher E. Hudson
Sean P. Huey
Doyle M. Hufstedler
Jamie L. Huggins
Eric R. Hull
Barton R. Humlhanz
Isaiah R. Hunt
Justin T. Hunt
Simeon Hunte
Joshua C. Hurley
James B. Huston Jr.
Seth Huston
Nolen R. Hutchings
Ray J. Hutchinson
Gregory P. Huxley Jr.
Benjamin W. Isenberg
Craig S. Ivory
Edward D. Iwan
Leslie D. Jackson
Marlon P. Jackson
Morgen N. Jacobs

Scott Jamar
Evan T. James
Luke S. James
William C. James
William A. Jeffries
Robert B. Jenkins
Troy David Jenkins
Darius T. Jennings
Ryan M. Jerabek
Linda C. Jimenez
Oscar Jiminez
Romulo J. Jiminez
Christopher B. Johnson
David W. Johnson
Howard Johnson II
John P. Johnson
Justin W. Johnson
Markus J. Johnson
Maurice J. Johnson
Michael Vann Johnson Jr.
Nathaniel H. Johnson
Paul J. Johnson
Philip A. Johnson Jr.
Rayshawn S. Johnson
Devon D. Jones
Gussie M. Jones
Raymond E. Jones Jr.
Rodney A. Jones
Kylan A. Jones-Huffman
Curt E. Jordan Jr.
Jason D. Jordan
Phillip A. Jordan
Forest J. Jostes
Spencer T. Karol
Michael G. Karr Jr.
Mark J. Kasecky
Jeffrey J. Kaylor
Chad L. Keith
Quinn A. Keith
Bryan P. Kelly
Brian Matthew Kennedy
Kyran E. Kennedy
Morgan D. Kennon
Christopher J. Kenny
Jonathan R. Kephart
Dallas L. Kerns
Erik C. Kesterson
Humayun S. M. Khan
James M. Kiehl
Shane E. Kielion
Jeungjin Na Kim
Kevin C. Kimmerly
Levi B. Kinchen
Lester O. Kinney II
David M. Kirchhoff
Charles A. Kiser
Nicholas Brian Kleiboeker
John K. Klinesmith Jr.
Floyd G. Knighten Jr.
Eric L. Knott
Joshua L. Knowles
Lance J. Koenig
Kevin T. Kolm
Martin W. Kondor
Patrick W. Kordsmeier
Edward J. Korn
Bradley S. Korthaus
Jakub Henryk Kowalik
Elmer C. Krause
Dustin L. Kreider
Bradley G. Kritzer
John F. Kurth
William W. Labadie Jr.
Joshua S. Ladd
Michael V. Lalush
Alan Dinh Lam
Jeffrey Lam
Charles R. Lamb
James I. Lambert III
James P. Lambert
Jonathan W. Lambert
Andrew David LaMont
Sean G. Landrus
Shawn A. Lane
Moises A. Langhorst
Sean M. Langley
Christopher J. Lapka
Tracy L. Laramore
Cole W. Larsen
Nicholas D. Larson
Scott Q. Larson Jr.
Matthew C. Laskowski
William T. Latham
Karina S. Lau
Jeffrey D. Lawrence
Mark A. Lawton
Travis J. Layfield
Rene Ledesma
Ryan Leduc
Bum R. Lee
Ken W. Leisten
Jerome Lemon
Cedric L. Lennon
Farao K. Letufuga
Justin W. Linden
Roger G. Ling
Joseph L. Lister
Nino D. Livaudais
Dale T. Lloyd
Daniel J. Londono
Ryan P. Long
Zachariah W. Long
Duane E. Longstreth
Edgar E. Lopez
Juan Lopez
Richard M. Lord
David L. Loyd
Victor R. Lu

Robert L. Lucero
Jason C. Ludlam
Jacob R. Lugo
John Lukac
Jason N. Lynch
Matthew D. Lynch
Christopher D. Mabry
Gregory E. MacDonald
Cesar F. Machado-Olmos
Vorn J. Mack
Joseph B. Maglione
Jarrod L. Maher
William J. Maher III
Dan T. Malcom Jr.
Toby W. Mallet
Ian D. Manuel
Pablo Manzano
Lyndon A. Marcus Jr.
Paul C. Mardis Jr.
Douglas Jose Marencoreyes
Jude C. Mariano
James E. Marshall
John W. Marshall
Ryan A. Martin
Stephen G. Martin
Francisco Martinez
Jesse J. Martinez
Michael A. Martinez
Oscar A. Martinez
Jacob D. Martir
Arthur S. Mastrapa
Johnny Villareal Mata
Ramon Mateo
James C. Matteson
Clint Richard Matthews
Matthew E. Matula
Donald C. May Jr.
Joseph P. Mayek
Patrick R. McCaffrey Sr.
Joseph C. McCarthy
Ryan M. McCauley
Daniel James McConnell
Brad P. McCormick
Erik S. McCrae
Donald R. McCune
Dustin K. McGaugh
Holly J. McGeogh
Brian D. McGinnis
Michael A. McGlothin
Scott R. McHugh
Joshua McIntosh
David M. McKeever
Eric S. McKinley
Robert L. McKinley
Justin D. McLeese
Don S. McMahan
Heath A. McMillin
Brian M. McPhillips
Jesus Martin Antonio Medellin
Brian A. Medina
Irving Medina
Oscar D. Medina
Kenneth A. Melton
Jaygee Meluat
Fernando A. Mendez-Aceves
Joseph Menusa
Eddie E. Menyweather
Gil Mercado
Michael M. Merila
Christopher A. Merville
Daniel K. Methvin
Jason M. Meyer
Eliu A. Miersandoval
Michael G. Mihalakis
Matthew G. Milczark
Jason David Mileo
Anthony S. Miller
Bruce Miller Jr.
Dennis J. Miller
Frederick L. Miller Jr.
Marvin L. Miller
William L. Miller
Joseph Minucci II
Troy L. Miranda
George A. Mitchell
Keman L. Mitchell
Michael W. Mitchell
Sean R. Mitchell
Jesse D. Mizener
Anthony W. Monroe
Adam G. Mooney
Horst G. Moore
Jason William Moore
Stuart W. Moore
Travis A. Moothart
Jose L. Mora
Melvin Y. Mora
Michael A. Mora
Kevin N. Morehead
Brent L. Morel
David J. Moreno
Gerardo Moreno
Jaime Moreno
Luis A. Moreno
Dennis B. Morgan
Richard L. Morgan Jr.
Geoffrey S. Morris
Ricky A. Morris Jr.
Nicholas B. Morrison
Shawna M. Morrison
Keelan L. Moss
Clifford L. Moxley Jr.
Cory R. Mracek
Rodney A. Murray
Krisna Nachampassak

Paul T. Nakamura
Nathan W. Nakis
Kenneth A. Nalley
Christopher G. Nason
Kevin G. Nave
Rafael L. Navea
Charles L. Neeley
Paul M. Neff II
Gavin L. Neighbor
Joshua M. Neusche
Joseph L. Nice
Dominique J. Nicolas
Isaac Michael Nieves
Patrick R. Nixon
Allen Nolan
Marcos O. Nolasco
William J. Normandy
Joseph C. Norquist
Byron W. Norwood
Leif E. Nott
Todd E. Nunes
David T. Nutt
Donald S. Oaks Jr.
Branden F. Oberleitner
Patrick T. O'Day
Shane K. O'Donnell
Charles E. Odums II
Ramon C. Ojeda
Brian Oliveira
Justin B. Onwordi
Richard P. Orengo
Kim S. Orlando
Eric J. Orlowski
Osbaldo Orozco
Cody J. Orr
Billy J. Orton
Pamela G. Osbourne
Deshon E. Otey
Kevin C. Ott
Michael C. Ottolini
Michael G. Owen
David Edward Owens Jr.
Fernando Padilla-Ramirez
Shawn D. Pahnke
Gabriel T. Palacios
Eric T. Paliwoda
Joshua D. Palmer
Joshua M. Palmer
Dale A. Panchot
Bradley L. Parker
Daniel R. Parker
James D. Parker
Tommy L. Parker Jr.
Harvey E. Parkerson III
David B. Parson
Esau G. Patterson Jr.
William L. Payne
George J. Payton
Michael F. Pedersen
Abraham D. Penamedina
Brian H. Penisten
Ross A. Pennanen
Gregory V. Pennington
Rafael Peralta
Andres H. Perez
Geoffrey Perez
Hector R. Perez
Joel Perez
Jose A. Perez III
Luis A. Perez
Nicholas Perez
Wilfredo Perez Jr.
Michael J. Pernaselli
David S. Perry
Charles C. Persing
Dustin W. Peters
Alyssa R. Peterson
Brett J. Petriken
James L. Pettaway Jr.
Erickson H. Petty
Jerrick M. Petty
Mark P. Phelan
Chance R. Phelps
Gladimir Philippe
Ivory L. Phipps
Pierre E. Piche
Aaron C. Pickering
Lori Ann Piestewa
Dennis L. Pintor
James H. Pirtle
Jason T. Poindexter
Frederick E. Pokorney Jr.
Andrew R. Pokorny
Justin W. Pollard
Larry E. Polley Jr.
Darrin K. Potter
David L. Potter
Christopher S. Potts
James E. Powell
Caleb J. Powers
Dean P. Pratt
Brian P. Prening
James E. Prevete
Kelley S. Prewitt
Tyler D. Prewitt
James W. Price
Timothy E. Price
Mathew D. Puckett
Jaror C. Puello-Coronado
Louis W. Qualls
Michael B. Quinn
Branden P. Ramey
Richard P. Ramey
Christopher Ramirez
Eric U. Ramirez
Gene Ramirez
William C. Ramirez
Christopher Ramos

Tamarra J. Ramos
Brandon Ramsey
Carson J. Ramsey
Edmond L. Randle
Cleston C. Raney
Marc M. Rapicault
Gregory A Ratzlaff
Rel A. Ravago IV
Omead H. Razani
Brandon M. Read
Christopher J. Reed
Ryan E. Reed
Tatjana Reed
Edward T. Reeder
Aaron T. Reese
Jeremy F. Regnier
Randall S. Rehn
Brendon C. Reiss
George S. Rentschler
Justin D. Reppuhn
Sean C. Reynolds
Rafael Reynosasuarez
Yadir G. Reynoso
Demetrius L. Rice
Ariel Rico
Jeremy L. Ridlen
Andrew G. Riedel
David G. Ries
Diego Fernando Rincon
Steven A. Rintamaki
Duane R. Rios
Russell B. Rippetoe
Henry C. Risner
Jose A. Rivera
John T. Rivero
Frank K. Rivers Jr.
Thomas D. Robbins
Todd J. Robbins
Anthony P. Roberts
Bob W. Roberts
Robert D. Roberts
Joseph E. Robsky Jr.
Moses D. Rocha
Marlin T. Rockhold
Jose Franci Gonzalez Rodriguez
Robert M. Rodriguez
Philip G. Rogers
Robert E. Rooney
Randal Kent Rosacker
Victor A. Rosaleslomeli
Richard H. Rosas
Scott C. Rose
Thomas C. Rosenbaum
Randy S. Rosenberg
Marco D. Ross
Lawrence A. Roukey
Alan Rowe
Brandon J. Rowe
Roger D. Rowe
Jonathan D. Rozier
Isela Rubalcava
Aaron J. Rusin
John W. Russell
Marc T. Ryan
Timothy Louis Ryan
Scott A. Saboe
Rasheed Sahib
Rudy Salas
William I. Salazar
Edward M. Saltz
Benjamin W. Sammis
Sonny G. Sampler
Gregory P. Sanders
Leroy Sandoval Jr.
Matthew J. Sandri
Barry Sanford Sr.
Neil Anthony Santoriello
Jonathan J. Santos
Brandon R. Sapp
Cameron B. Sarno
Scott D. Sather
Jeremiah E. Savage
Michael P. Scarborough
Robert C. Scheetz Jr.
Justin B. Schmidt
Jeremiah W. Schmunk
Sean M. Schneider
Dustin H. Schrage
Mathew E. Schram
Brian K. Schramm
Christian C. Schulz
David A. Scott
Kerry D. Scott
Stephen M. Scott
Juan E. Segura
Marc S. Seiden
Christopher Scott Seifert
Dustin M. Sekula
Matthew K. Serio
Juan M. Serrano
Wentz Jerome Henry Shanaberger III
Jeffrey R. Shaver
Kevin M. Shea
Casey Sheehan
Kevin F. Sheehan
Daniel Michael Shepherd
Alan D. Sherman
Anthony L. Sherman
Jonathan B. Shields
Harry N. Shondee Jr.
Brad S. Shuder
James A. Shull
Kenneth L. Sickels
Dustin L. Sides
Erik H. Silva
Sean A. Silva

Leonard D. Simmons
Abraham Simpson
Charles M. Sims
John T. Sims Jr.
Sean P. Sims
Uday Singh
Aaron J. Sissel
Christopher A. Sisson
David Sisung
Nicholas M. Skinner
Brian D. Slavenas
Russell L. Slay
Brandon U. Sloan
Richard P. Slocum
Thomas J. Slocum
Corey L. Small
Keith L. Smette
Antoine D. Smith
Benedict J. Smith
Benjamin K. Smith
Brandon C. Smith
Brian D. Smith
Bruce A. Smith
Darrell L. Smith
Edward Smith
Eric A. Smith
Jeremiah D. Smith
Matthew R. Smith
Michael J. Smith Jr.
Orenthial J. Smith
Paul R. Smith
Christopher F. Soelzer
Roderic A. Solomon
Adrian V. Soltau
Charles R. Soltes Jr.
Armando Soriano
Tomas Sotelo Jr.
Kenneth C. Souslin
Philip I. Spakosky
Jason L. Sparks
Michael R. Speer
Trevor Spink
Christopher J. Splinter
Marvin R. Sprayberry III
Bryan N. Spry
Michael B. Stack
Nathan E. Stahl
Andrew K. Stern
Robert A. Stever
Gregory Stone
Matthew R. Stovall
Morgan W. Strader
William R. Strange
Kirk Allen Straseskie
Brandon C. Sturdy
William R. Sturges Jr.
Paul J. Sturino
Jesus A. Suarez Del Solar
Joseph D. Suell
John R. Sullivan
Narson B. Sullivan
Vincent M. Sullivan
Ernest Harold Sutphin
Michael J. Sutter
James E. Swain
Sharon T. Swartworth
Thomas J. Sweet II
Christopher W. Swisher
Paul R. Syverson III
Patrick S. Tainsh
DeForest L. Talbert
Linda Ann Tarango-Griess
Michael Yury Tarlavsky
Christopher M. Taylor
Mark D. Taylor
John R. Teal
Riayan A. Tejeda
Jason Andrew Tetrault
Joseph C. Thibodeaux
Thomas R. Thigpen Sr.
Jesse L. Thiry
Carl Thomas
Kendall Thomas
Kyle G. Thomas
Anthony O. Thompson
Jarrett B. Thompson
Lance M. Thompson
Robert C. Thornton Jr.
Humberto F. Timoteo
John E. Tipton
Joshua K. Titcomb
Brandon T. Titus
Brandon S. Tobler
Lee D. Todacheene
John H. Todd III
Nicholas A. Tomko
Timothy Toney
George D. Torres
Michael S. Torres
Ramon Reyes Torres
Richard Torres
Elias Torrez III
Michael L. Tosto
Quoc Binh Tran
Richard K. Trevithick
John B. Trotter
Andrew L. Tuazon
Roger C. Turner Jr.
Scott M. Tyrrell
Andre D. Tyson
Eugene A. Uhl III
Drew M. Uhles
Rick A. Ulbright
Daniel P. Unger
Robert Oliver Unruh
Ernest E. Utt
Michael A. Uvanni
Gary A. Vaillant

Ruben Valdez Jr.
Melissa Valles
Brian K. Van Dusen
Allen J. Vandayburg
Josiah H. Vandertulip
John J. Vangyzen IV
Gary F. VanLeuven
Oscar D. Vargas-Medina
Mark D. Vasquez
Frances M. Vega
Michael W. Vega
Paul A. Velazquez
Jose A. Velez
David M. Vicente
Joselito O. Villanueva
Scott M. Vincent
Kimberly A. Voelz
Michael S. Voss
Thai Vue
Michael B. Wafford
Christopher A. Wagener
Gregory L. Wahl
Allan K. Walker
Jeffery C. Walker
Donald R. Walters
Jason M. Ward
Robert P. Warns II
Nachez Washalanta
Christopher B. Wasser
David L. Waters
Kendall Damon Waters-Bey
William R. Watkins III
Christopher E. Watts
Aaron A. Weaver
Charles J. Webb
Michael S. Weger
David J. Weisenburg
Douglas J. Weismantle
Michael Russell Creighton Weldon
Larry L. Wells
Lonny D. Wells
Stephen M. Wells
Cody L. Wentz
Jeffrey M. Wershow
Christopher J. Rivera Wesley
James G. West
Phillip G. West
Alexander E. Wetherbee
Donald L. Wheeler
Mason Douglas Whetstone
Marquis A. Whitaker
Aaron Dean White
Nathan D. White
Raymond L. White
Steven W. White
William W. White
Joey D. Whitener
Chase R. Whitham
Michael J. Wiesemann
Joshua S. Wilfong
Charles L. Wilkins III
Eugene Williams
Michael J. Williams
Michael L. Williams
Taft V. Williams
Christopher R. Willoughby
Dana N. Wilson
Jerry L. Wilson
Joe N. Wilson
Lamont N. Wilson
Nicholas Wilt
Ronald Winchester
Trevor A. Wine
William J. Wiscowiche
Clinton L. Wisdom
Robert A. Wise
Michelle M. Witmer
Owen D. Witt
James R. Wolf
Jeremy L. Wolfe
Elijah Tai Wah Wong
Brian M. Wood
George A. Wood
Nathan R. Wood
Michael R. Woodliff
Julian Woods
James C. Wright
Jason G. Wright
John T. Wroblewski
Luke C. Wullenwaber
Daniel R. Wyatt
Stephen E. Wyatt
Michael E. Yashinski
Henry Ybarra III
Justin R. Yoemans
Rodricka A. Youmans
Ryan C. Young
Andrew J. Zabierek
Nicholas J. Zangara
Robert J. Zangas
Mark Anthony Zapata
Thomas J. Zapp
Nicholaus E. Zimmer
Nicholas L. Ziolkowski
Ian T. Zook
Robert P. Zurheide Jr.

This list represents the fallen through November 19, 2004

WOW VOWS

J.Lo, Tiger, Kevin Costner and Billy Joel all got spliced, but for sheer surprise and over-the-top style, Britney took the wedding cake

GREETINGS! The 27 guests were totally in the dark until they received these pink cards upon arrival at the friend's home where the wedding took place.

Britney Spears and Kevin Federline

The Celebration: Jumping the gun by a month on her intended October wedding date, Britney and her dancer boyfriend, 26, provided a joyous jolt for invitees to what they believed to be an engagement party in Studio City, California.

The Prequel: At 5:30 a.m. on January 3, Spears had married her Kentwood, Louisiana, homeboy Jason Allen Alexander at the Little White Wedding Chapel in Las Vegas only to get it annulled 55 hours later.

Surprise!

It is with much love that we welcome you to our Wedding Ceremony

Tonight

Saturday, the eighteenth of September Two thousand and four at eight o'clock in the evening

Britney & Kevin

NATTY NUPS: Brit chose a $26,000 strapless silk Monique Lhuillier, while Kevin looked stud-ious in a tux by Jeff Fox at Scott Hill.

TOTALLY MATRIMONIAL: Britney's "Maids" changed from $3,000 Monique Lhuillier gowns into hot pink Juicy Couture sweats (below); mom Lynne (seated lower right) was designated "Hot Mama." Kevin's father, Mike (above, far left), and stepdad, Coby Bleak (far right), shared fatherly designations, while the madcap groom stepped out as "The Pimp" with his Juicy-clad groomsmen.

DIAMONDS AND LACE: Delicately woven half gloves (Brit's idea) complemented her 5-carat rock (below) and Sergio Rossi sandals (above).

Tears for Spears: "I lost it," recalled Federline. "I remember looking over at her mom, and we both started to cry."

The Heat: "I just wanted to holler, 'Get a room!'" said a bridesmaid after they passionately sealed the deal. "It was such a big kiss."

What's Next: "I can see myself as a mom," said the bride. "At 23, I am so there."

SWITCH HIT: "I was hot in my wedding dress," said Brit, who changed into an even hotter Lhuillier to cut the white chocolate butter cake.

Kevin Costner and Christine Baumgartner

Field of Dreams: The outdoor enthusiasts tied the knot on his 165-acre ranch outside Aspen.

Rocky Mountain: Baumgartner, 30, a handbag designer, wore a 5-carat diamond-set wedding ring designed by Neil Lane.

Marriage Material: The groom, 49, donned a classic Ralph Lauren cashmere suit, while the bride chose a ruched satin gown with hand-made roses designed by Monique Lhuillier.

Notable Guests: Bruce Willis, Tim Allen, Don Johnson, Robert Wagner, Clay Walker

The Return of Bruno's Heartbeat: Rehearsal dinner guests were treated to a surprise jam session featuring both Willis and Johnson.

The couple beamed in front of the antique truck used to transport the bride and her father, Jim, to the floral altar and an awaiting Costner.

Tori Spelling and Charlie Shanian

Extravaganza: The Badgley Mischka-clad bride, 31, and actor-writer Shanian, 35, enjoyed a $1 million bash at her folks' 56,000-sq.-ft. Los Angeles manse. Wolfgang Puck handled the food while guests toasted and tippled from a champagne fountain in a rose-covered gazebo.

The Peach Pit Meets *The Love Boat*: The 350 attendees included a mix of *90210* alums (Ian Ziering, Jennie Garth, Jason Priestley) and long-time friends of the Spelling family (Ed McMahon, Jackie Collins).

Gifted Kids: The pair began receiving presents from strangers as soon as their registries (Tiffany and Williams-Sonoma) hit the Web.

The mixed-faith couple—she's Jewish, he's Christian—incorporated traditions from both in the ceremony.

JULY 3

Bob Guiney and Rebecca Budig

Just Bob: Guiney, 33, is Bachelor Bob no more, marrying *All My Children* actress Budig, 31, after a brief six-week engagement.

Misty-Eyed: The bride, in a strapless blue gown, and groom, wearing an open-neck shirt and cargo pants, opted for casual nuptials near his family's Long Lake, Michigan, cottage. After wiping away tears of joy during the ceremony, the duo donned swimsuits for an afternoon of activities on the water.

G Is for Gift: The couple made sure none of the guests left empty-handed, with everyone receiving a knit hat with a "G" (for Guiney) on the front and "7-3-04" on the back.

"They're very smitten with each other," Budig's mother, Mary, said of the newlyweds.

Star Jones and Al Reynolds

"I have been to a lot of beautiful weddings, but that one took the cake," said Vivica A. Fox, one of 12 bridesmaids.

Catch a Falling Star: It was love at first sight when the *View* cohost, 42, and her banker beau, 34, hooked up at a party a year earlier. Sharing with the world, they set up a Web site to chronicle the relationship, which, said *The View*'s Meredith Vieira, has made her "kinder and gentler."

Big Deal: 450 guests watched the bride's Cinderella moment as she trailed a 27-foot crystal-encrusted veil for her walk down the aisle at a New York church. Next stop: the "opulent, palace, fantasy, fairy-tale" fete, as described by party planner David Tutera, at the Waldorf-Astoria.

Celebrity Views: In addition to her gabfest gal pals, notable attendees included Senator Hillary Clinton, Donald Trump, Samuel L. Jackson, Spike Lee, Chris Rock and Kim Cattrall.

OCTOBER 2

Billy Joel and Katie Lee

Piano Man: His own wedding singer, Joel, 55, serenaded his bride, 23, in a 45-minute, 20-song set "until we dragged him away," said the event planner.

New York State of Mind: Joel transformed a party tent on his oceanfront Long Island estate into a farmhouse, with faux shutters, windowsills and hanging vines. Lee, an aspiring TV chef, helped prepare the Tuscan-themed wedding feast.

Backstage Passes: Guests included Howard Stern, Paul Reiser, Jimmy Webb and Joel's second ex, Christie Brinkley.

Stepmom Bonding: "We almost have a sisterly bond," Lee said of Billy's 19-year-old daughter with Brinkley, Alexa Ray, the maid of honor.

The bride easily stood a head taller than the groom in her Jimmy Choo heels, custom Oscar de la Renta gown and borrowed 50-carat diamond necklace.

January 1
Singer **Lou Rawls,** 71, and flight attendant **Nina Malek Inman,** 34.

January 24
Actress **Selma Blair,** 32, and **Ahmet Zappa,** 30, Frank's actor-rocker son.

April 1
Fear Factor couple **Chris Jackson,** 28, and **Monica Gonzales,** 25, in vows conse-crated by the show's host, Joe Rogan, who had gotten himself ordained online.

April 4
Grammy winner **Beck,** 36, and actress **Marissa Ribisi,** 30.

April 17
The Satanic Verses author **Salman Rushdie,** 57, and wife No. 4, model-actress **Padma Lakshmi,** 34.

April 29
Oscar-winning actress **Celeste Holm,** 85, and opera singer **Frank Basile,** 41.

May 23
Platinum-selling singer **Michelle Branch,** 21, and her bassist **Teddy Landau,** 40.

May 29
Actress/*SNL* alum **Molly Shannon,** 40, and artist **Fritz Chesnut,** 31.

June 19
The King of Queens' **Kevin James,** 39, and model **Steffiana De La Cruz,** 30.

July 2
Oscar-winning actress **Mira Sorvino,** 37, and actor **Christopher Backus,** 23. Her actor dad, Paul, saluted them with Neapolitan ballads at the reception.

AUGUST 7

Fred Savage and Jennifer Stone

Love at Second Sight: The pair were neighbors in suburban Chicago until Savage moved, at 11, to L.A. to star as winsome Kevin Arnold in *The Wonder Years.* They reconnected at a fete in 1999 for Savage's 23rd birthday. "We started talking and smooching," recalled the groom, "and we've been together ever since."
Deal Sealer: "Seeing Fred at the end of the aisle was the best part," declared Stone, 31, a commercial real estate agent. The wedding took place at Los Angeles's flower-festooned L'Orangerie restaurant.
Wedding Vows: "I promised to always bring up a glass of water to her before we go to bed," said Savage, 28, last seen in *Welcome to Mooseport* and turning to directing. "She promised to never let me dress myself."

"I had tears, but they were tears of joy," said Stone, who'd lost touch with Savage during his run on *The Wonder Years* and studies at Stanford.

OCTOBER 5

Tiger Woods and Elin Nordegren

Course Closed: Woods took over all 112 rooms of the exclusive Sandy Lane resort in Barbados for 10 days so his Swedish bride, former nanny and model Nordegren, 24, could chill with pals. He arrived two days before the sunset, Caribbean-side ceremony.
In the Gallery: Fellow sports legends Michael Jordan and Charles Barkley were among 120 guests lapping up caviar, champagne and tunes by Hootie and the Blowfish.
The Purse: The tab came to $2 million, not including the two-week honeymoon of Woods, 29, and Nordegren on his $22 million yacht *Privacy.*
Iron Nerves: Woods, it was reported, "didn't act like he was going to get married. He was very relaxed, like this was any other day."

Sandy Lane has three golf courses, but Woods spent the pre-wedding morning jet-skiing and snorkeling.

July 4
Actor **Dennis Quaid**, 50, and wife No. 3, real estate agent **Kimberly Buffington**, 33.

July 30
Oscar winner **Nicolas Cage**, 40, and his third, former sushi waitress **Alice Kim**, 20.

August 15
Actress **Diane Lane**, 39, and actor **Josh Brolin**, 36. Guests included his actor dad, James, and stepmom, Barbra Streisand, plus the bride's child and the groom's two.

August 28
Law & Order: SVU's **Mariska Hargitay**, 40, and actor **Peter Hermann**, 37.

September 4
Louise Brown, 26, the world's first test-tube baby, and bank security officer **Wesley Mullinder**, 33, in England.

September 9
'N Sync's **Joey Fatone**, 27, and his high school sweetheart, actress **Kelly Baldwin**, 28.

October 2
Sitcom star **Katey Sagal**, 50, and **Kurt Sutter**, 44, producer-writer of *The Shield*.

JUNE 5

Jennifer Lopez and Marc Anthony

"This time she didn't need to have a big, fancy wedding," said a friend. "She just wanted to get married to the man she loved."

The Wedding Planner: With plenty of practice off-camera and on, J.Lo, 35, had invited about 35 guests to her Beverly Hills home for a "beautiful afternoon party" that turned out to be her third stroll down the aisle. She wore a ruffled Vera Wang, he Armani.

The Bling: Except for her 7.36-carat starburst diamond solitaire Chopard ring, Lopez's $7 million of glitter was on loan from Neil Lane.

Life of the Party: Lopez's mom, Guadalupe, was so pleased that Jenny from the Block was marrying Anthony, 36, that she entered the reception tent doing "a little shimmy, shaking her booty," according to a witness.

Testimonial: Though they were together for only four months and he had just divorced Dayanara Torres, the couple dated in 1998. This time, said a friend, "they didn't need any more time to make up their minds."

SPLIT DECISIONS

Adieu to Bennifer, and to Tom and his Penélope, who burned bright but briefly. And to all the uncoupled, including that long-inseparable pair who were molded for each other, Barbie and Ken

Everything was ready for the Wedding of the Century, right down to the invitations designed to match the bride's silver Rolls Royce and the Lalique crystal figurine table decorations symbolizing lasting love. Bridesmaids would wear and keep $12,000 pink sapphire heart necklaces from Neil Lane; groomsmen, nifty $15,000 DeGrisogono watches. There was also, of course, the $1.2 million, 6.1-carat Harry Winston engagement ring and the prepaid, nonrefundable $2 million price tag for what turned out to be The Wedding That Never Was. When the celebrated couple known as Bennifer called off their long-anticipated Santa Barbara, California, nuptials just four days before the big event, they blamed the media tsunami that had engulfed them. Though they then made plans for a somewhat more modest fete a few weeks later on Affleck's $7.1 million Georgia island estate—preparations included getting the FAA to declare a no-fly zone over the property to thwart airborne paparazzi—his heart was no longer in it. "Jennifer didn't realize it at that moment, but when he called [the first wedding] off, the relationship was over," said a friend of theirs. "He got out of the trap, and he wasn't going to get back in. He was looking for a graceful way to let it die." The conclusion came in January, when Lopez's rep announced it was over. And we bid bye-bye to Bennifer, Hollywood's most epic coupling since Liz & Dick. After meeting two years before on the set of their disastrous flick *Gigli,* Ben and Jen became The Item, with nonstop coverage of their public embraces and spats, their lavish spendathons, his nights carousing with strippers and gambling into the wee hours. Reported to be "hysterical and very deeply depressed" in the aftermath, Jenny, 35, was soon back on the block, and at the altar, with salsa star Marc Anthony, while Affleck, 32, created a new, quieter Bennifer with an at-least-interim lady, Jennifer Garner. As for the original model, it was, as their wedding planner said of the nixed nuptials, "a wonderful adventure."

Ben Affleck and Jennifer Lopez

HOT COUPLE, COLD FEET: "They're different," a mutual friend said of the pair. Another pal pointed out that while she liked to hit the sack early, he very much enjoyed the nightlife: "It was hard to merge their two lifestyles."

Smile hard: The couple enjoyed a happy moment at the L.A. premiere of *The Whole Ten Yards*.

Bruce Willis and Brooke Burns

Though their nine-month courtship reached its final destination in May, the slick-headed screen fixture and former *Baywatch* beauty did rack up a ton of frequent-flyer miles along the way. Shortly after their first date in August 2003, the couple packed up for a Costa Rican beach getaway. From there they moved on to higher-profile appearances, serving up public displays of affection at a New York Yankees World Series game, the Radio Music Awards in Vegas, a joint birthday party in L.A. and even at the Louvre during a weeklong jaunt in Paris. Although Willis, 49, and Burns, 26, purchased matching Cartier plain platinum wedding bands while in the City of Light, reps insist they were never engaged. Clearly the pair enjoyed covering distances together, but the flame flickered out after Burns flew solo to shoot her TV series *North Shore* in Hawaii.

Rebecca Romijn-Stamos and John Stamos

One of Hollywood's most photogenic couples since they hooked up at a Victoria's Secret fashion show in 1994, the model turned actress, 32, and former *Full House* star, 41, announced that they were amicably ending their 5½-year marriage. They acknowledged having difficulties since 2003 but couldn't fix them, given her far-flung filming schedule and his re-rooting on Broadway. "It's sad and it's painful," said Romijn-Stamos. "I'm still trying to get my head around it." But within a few months, she had resumed using her maiden name and begun dating *Crossing Jordan*'s Jerry O'Connell. And Stamos looked forward to finding another woman who would have him crying, in the words of his *Full House* character, "Have mercy." "I'm making a prediction," he said. "I will be married within the next year and a half to two years. I'm going to the next part of my life." Any takers?

Fall guy: Meister served as the handbag designer's latest disposable accessory following their nuptials.

Nicky Hilton and Todd Meister

Their August weekend in Las Vegas got rolling with Tara Reid leading the gang in a round of Lemon Drop shots and climaxed with big sister Paris as maid of honor at an impromptu 2:30 a.m. rite at the Vegas Wedding Chapel. But, like Reid, who sprang into the Palms resort pool fully clothed, the younger Hilton, 21, and money manager Meister, 34, should have looked before they plunged. Meister, a pal for five years, had proposed just a few weeks earlier. The quickie ceremony caught family members (except for Paris) off guard. "They were dating off and on, but this was out of the blue," said Francesca Hilton, her great aunt. So, two months later, was their split. Nicky returned the ring, once worn by Meister's mom, and the only financial impact of the fiasco was the more than $1,000 blown on the wedding.

"We looked at each other and it was like right out of a stupid movie," Stamos once said. "I fell stone head-over-heels in love."

BYE-BYE LOVES

American Idol's **Paula Abdul,** 42, and Smith & Wesson Holding Corp. director **Colton Melby,** 53, split nine months after being introduced by the elite L.A. matchmaker Kelleher & Associates.

Two and a Half Men's **Jon Cryer,** 39, and his wife, actress **Sarah Trigger,** 36, after four years.

24's **Kiefer Sutherland,** 38, filed for divorce from model **Elizabeth Kelly Winn,** 43, after being separated for five of their eight years together.

Tennis stars **Kim Clijsters,** 21, and **Lleyton Hewitt,** 23, ended their love match at four years.

NBA star **Rick Fox,** 35, and former Miss America **Vanessa Williams,** 41, divorced after five years.

Metallica drummer **Lars Ulrich,** 41, and wife **Skylar,** 33, after keeping time for seven years.

Today's **Katie Couric,** 47, and TV producer **Tom Werner,** 54, four years after they met on a blind date.

Music scions **Sean Lennon,** 29, and **Bijou Phillips,** 24, after four years.

The Sopranos' **Edie Falco,** 41, and her Broadway costar **Stanley Tucci,** 44, after nearly a year.

Barbie and Ken

They were the very picture of the perfect couple. Even after 43 years as boyfriend and girlfriend, they never stopped smiling. Theirs was a relationship based on trust and the mutual respect of two individuals, both comfortable in their own plastic skin. So it came as a shock when, two days before Valentine's Day, Mattel Inc. announced that Barbie and Ken were kaput. Fans of the couple were bewildered. "Who will get the Dream House?" worried a *New York Times* writer. Barbie, who debuted as a fashion model in 1959, and Ken, who strutted stiff-legged to life two years later, never wed nor bred. The two "will always remain the best of friends," said a Mattel spokesman, not denying whispers that Barbie was displaying keen interest in surfing and in a hunky Aussie boogie-board-riding doll named Blaine. No comment from Ken.

Andie MacDowell and Rhett Hartzog

At the reception following their fairy-tale wedding, the band played "What a Wonderful World." And so it seemed when the actress wed an old high school classmate from Gaffney, South Carolina. MacDowell's three kids with former model Paul Qualley participated in the ceremony, lighting a unity candle with their new stepfather, an Atlanta jewelry salesman. The couple settled in Asheville, North Carolina, but divorced just three years later. "It's hard combining families," MacDowell's sister Babs explained. As for MacDowell, 46, "I have no bad feelings toward Rhett," she said, "and wish him only happiness." Added a friend of the couple: "They just parted ways. Fairy tales don't always come true."

"It's unfortunate," said Hartzog (with MacDowell). "Both tried," said her sister. "We're all sad about it."

The breakup was described as "amicable" by Cruise's sister Lee Anne DeVette, who doubles as his publicist.

Tom Cruise and Penélope Cruz

"It's always the little things I like in a relation-ship," said Cruise, 42, meaning that he was fond of pampering his girlfriend by cooking romantic dinners and drawing her baths. In the end, though, it was a *big* thing that left Cruz, 30, going it alone in the tub: Most of their time in the relationship was spent apart. "It's hard day to day not to see your partner," Cruz's rep said. "They were always making movies." In fact, the two actaholics shot 13 films between them in the three years since they met on the set of *Vanilla Sky,* keeping a schedule that can only be called romance-curdling or -encouraging. On the Morocco location for her upcoming release *Sahara,* Cruz launched a liaison with costar Matthew McConaughey.

Jesse Palmer and Jessica Bowlin

Six weeks before he reported to New York Giants summer training camp, the Bachelor and his law-student sweetheart benched their relationship during a cross-country long-distance call. While the conversation led to a few tears on her end in L.A., the decision was ultimately mutual. "We decided that we wanted to move forward as friends rather than romantically," said Palmer, 26. "Obviously distance played a role." Bowlin, 22, agreed: "Not being able to spend a lot of time together was probably the toughest thing." Despite the show's idyllic premise, their breakup left *The Bachelor* pairings with an 0-for-5 success rate. Unlike previous contestants, the only item Palmer bestowed during the final rose ceremony was a one-way plane ticket that, he later noted, hadn't been used. "She's always got an invitation to come see a game or hang out for a weekend," he said. But they might want to add a return leg on the flight.

Naomi Watts and Heath Ledger

Ah, youth. That's the curse Watts, 36, blamed when she and her 25-year-old boyfriend went bust. Tales emerged of a spat in a Los Angeles club where she became furious over his flirting with 19-year-old Scarlett Johansson. It only got worse after Ledger was reported stealing kisses with Winona Ryder at a party. The two Aussies had met on the set of *Ned Kelly* in 2002 and stayed together through the 2004 Oscars, where she was a Best Actress nominee for *21 Grams*. Yet finally Watts gave up on the party-hearty lad she decided was "too immature." But she left with only kind sentiments: "I have nothing but good things to say about my romance with Heath. We loved each other. I'm close with his family; he's close with mine. He is a friend, and we'll always remain in contact." As for returning to the market, Watts indicated that she was in no rush, adding, "I'm not going to run after it."

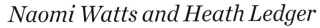

The matchup of pro quarterback Palmer and aspiring lawyer Bowlin resulted in an incomplete pass.

"People don't recognize me," Watts said of her welcome lowered profile since the SAG Awards (above). "It was different when I was with Heath."

Teen mogul **Ashley Olsen,** 18, and Columbia University quarterback **Matt Kaplan,** 20, after three steady years.

Up in smoke after 20 years: Cheech & Chong's **Cheech Marin,** 58, and wife **Patti,** 52.

Above Average Joe **Adam Mesh,** 20, and saleswoman **Samantha Trenk,** 24, after two months.

White Chicks' **Keenen Ivory Wayans,** 46, and wife **Daphne,** 33, after 15 years.

Robert Downey Jr., 39, and wife **Deborah Falconer,** 39, after 12 tumultuous years.

It girl **Brittany Murphy,** 27, and talent manager **Jeff Kwatinetz,** 39, after 13 months.

Hip-hop wag **Snoop Dogg,** 33, and wife **Shanté,** 29, after seven years.

Oscar winner **Halle Berry,** 38, and husband **Eric Benét**, 38, after three years.

Radio force **Rush Limbaugh,** 53, and **Marta,** 45, his wife of 10 years.

TLC's **T-Boz,** 34, and rapper husband **Mack 10,** 33, after four years.

Flamboyant Harlem politician **Rev. Al Sharpton,** 50, and **Kathy Lee Jordan,** 48, his wife of more than 20 years.

STORK

Apple Blythe Alison | May 14

GWYNETH PALTROW & CHRIS MARTIN

Paltrow, 32, spent 70 grueling hours in labor awaiting the birth of the intercontinental couple's first child. Coldplay frontman Martin, 27, played the supportive husband by writing the Oscar winner a silly song which included lyrics like "I'll be there with you, baby, through the thin and the thick, I'm gonna clean up all the poo and the sick." While the baby's middle names honor her grandmothers, Blythe Danner and Alison Martin, the couple insist her fruity moniker has no special significance. "It's just a very cool name," said the proud papa.

Coco Riley | June 13

COURTENEY COX & DAVID ARQUETTE

Barely five weeks after the *Friends* finale aired, Cox, 40, got started on her own spinoff with husband Arquette, 33. The healthy 6-lb. girl was a joyous conclusion to three trying years of miscarriages and failed attempts at in vitro fertilization. "There's nobody I can think of who has wanted to be a mother as much as she has and will make as good of a mother as she will," said *Friends* executive producer David Crane. "She's one of the most nurturing people I've ever met."

The big bird earned his frequent-flyer miles this year, delivering a Coco for Courteney, a Ryder for Kate, a Marina for Matt and an Apple for Gwyneth's eye. Talk about the fruit of the luminous

TALES

OTHER BIRTHS

Makena Lei Gordon | May 13

HELEN HUNT & MATTHEW CARNAHAN It was as good as it gets for Hunt, 41, when she and her TV producer-writer boyfriend Carnahan, 43, welcomed their not-quite-6-lb. daughter. Days after the couple returned from a Hawaiian vacation, the little island girl was born four weeks early at Los Angeles's Cedars-Sinai. Their first child was named after a favorite town on Maui and Hunt's father, TV director Gordon Hunt. The Oscar winner gained just 25 lbs. during the pregnancy, thanks in part to a regular yoga routine.

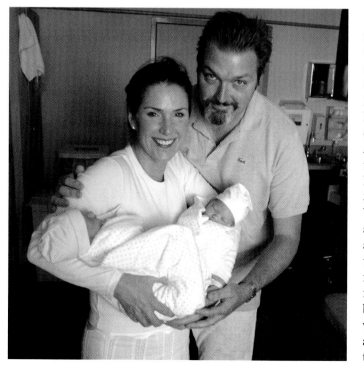

Stella and Ava | May 7

PERI GILPIN & CHRISTIAN VINCENT Accustomed to dealing with the whiny Crane brothers as *Frasier's* Roz Doyle, Gilpin, 43, now has a new set of siblings demanding her attention. After years of failed in vitro treatments, the actress and her artist husband, Vincent, 38, turned to a surrogate. When the 17½-in.-long Stella and 19-in.-long Ava finally arrived in a Nevada hospital, the couple burbled simultaneously that holding their new girls was "the best, best, best in the world, world, world." Guess they're already used to repeating themselves.

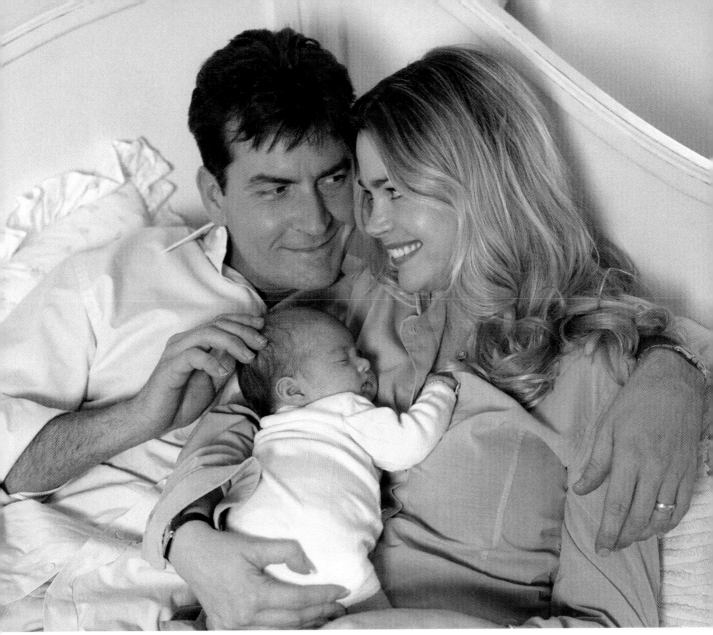

Sam | March 9

CHARLIE SHEEN & DENISE RICHARDS It's taken years for Sheen, 39, to shed his bad-boy rep, but considering the actor's devoted relationship with actress Richards, 33, and the impact of his 7-lb. 3-oz. daughter, he appears to be redefining the term "ladies' man." His first words after the C-section delivery, said Richards, were "Oh, little princess." Unlike many famous peers, the couple decided to keep it simple when choosing a name. "Some of these celebrity names today are way out there," said Sheen. "It might be cool for a parent to introduce Binocular Jones when he's 6 months old, but in school, it's sort of a curse."

Ryder Russell | January 7

KATE HUDSON & CHRIS ROBINSON Hudson, 25, and her rocker husband, 38, named their firstborn, an 8-lb. 11-oz. boy, to recognize both Dad's song "Ride" and the Grateful Dead's "I Know You, Rider." "It's the most incredible thing, but nobody ever tells you how hard it's gonna be," said the actress, who dropped 60 lbs. of baby weight in four months through a rigid diet and daily three-hour workouts. Expectations are high for the little guy. "I can't wait to see what he turns into," said actor Kurt Russell, Hudson's stepdad.

Roman Walker | April 7

DEBRA MESSING & DANIEL ZELMAN She had to camouflage her swelling belly during much of last season's *Will & Grace* and then miss the final four episodes altogether when she was put on bed rest. But after the arrival of Roman, Messing and her actor-writer husband, Zelman, 37, couldn't hide their joy. "I did nothing but breast-feed and spend day and night gazing into my son's eyes," said the first-time mom, 36. In August it was back to work for mother—and child, as Roman took up residence in a nursery built next to Messing's dressing room. "He gets lots of attention," reported *W&G* guest star Janet Jackson. "He's adorable."

Marina Pearl | February 8

MATT LeBLANC & MELISSA McKNIGHT The baby's timing was impeccable. LeBlanc, 37, had just finished shooting the last episode of *Friends* and was getting ready for the NBC follow-up, *Joey,* when Marina made her entrance. It was his own first child, but he knew the drill from parenting Tyler, 14, and Jacqueline, 10, the kids of McKnight, 39, during their five-year courtship. LeBlanc hadn't had much diapering practice but quickly got up to speed. "I'm pretty good at it now," he noted after three months. "It's like a little NASCAR pit stop."

Catherine Rose | March 8

CHERYL HINES & PAUL YOUNG Giving up work and cocktail outings for a while didn't hurt. Nor did labor, thanks to the epidural. Also her mom, Rosemary Harbolt, moved in from Florida for the first month to help the *Curb Your Enthusiasm* star, 39, and producer Young, 35. So all in all, parenthood proved a pleasant surprise. "People say, 'Everything you know is going to change,' so we were bracing for the worst," said Hines. "It's much less a sacrifice than I thought it would be."

Leni | May 4

HEIDI KLUM & FLAVIO BRIATORE "She loves me singing about her poop," Klum, 31, said of her daughter. "All I want to do is make her laugh." The German model, who'd split from Italian businessman Briatore, 54, back in January, didn't waste time returning to life's runway. In short order she lost 30 lbs. and gained a new guy, singer Seal. "People say, 'Oh, [with a newborn] you're in pain and you're tired and you can't have sex and everything is miserable,'" said Klum. "For me... it's the opposite. I guess I am lucky."

BEST & WORST DRESSED

Can we frock? It was a year of frills that thrilled, as begowned beauties floated down the red carpet. Nicole looked cool in sea foam, Renée reigned in ruffles, and Beyoncé went with the glow. And the year's perps of fashion faux pas should take a cue from exemplars of chic like Charlize

CHARLIZE THERON
On Oscar night, the Best Actress winner (for *Monster*) glittered in a beaded body-hugger from Tom Ford's final collection for Gucci.

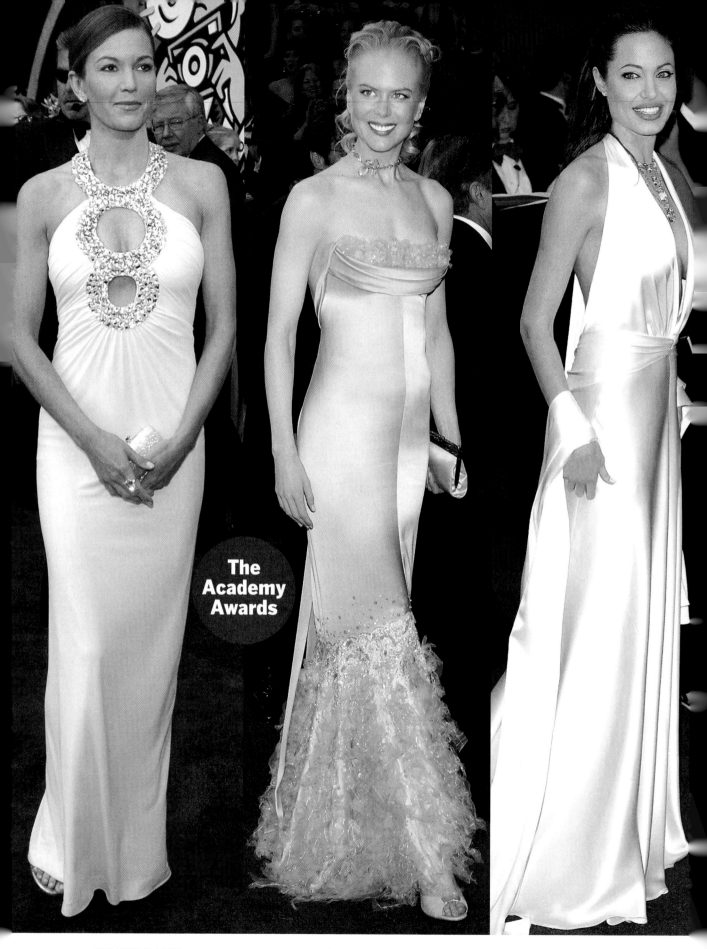

The Academy Awards

DIANE LANE
in Loris Azzaro

NICOLE KIDMAN
in Chanel

ANGELINA JOLIE
in Marc Bouwer

NAOMI WATTS
in Atelier Versace

OPRAH WINFREY
in Gianfranco Ferre

JULIA ROBERTS
in Giorgio Armani

The
Golden
Globe
Awards

CATE BLANCHETT
in Donna Karan

PATRICIA CLARKSON
in Bill Blass

UMA THURMAN
in Versace

JENNIFER ANISTON
in vintage Valentino

CHARLIZE THERON
in Christian Dior

KRISTIN DAVIS
in Prada

HOLLY HUNTER
in Vera Wang

ALLISON JANNEY
in Vera Wang

CATHERINE ZETA-JONES
in Elie Saab

The Screen Actors Guild Awards

LIV TYLER
in Marc Jacobs

DEBRA MESSING
in Elie Saab

RENEE ZELLWEGER
in Carolina Herrera

SCARLETT JOHANSSON
in Calvin Klein

LUCY LIU
in Emanuel Ungaro

HILARY SWANK
in Calvin Klein

The
Costume
Institute
Gala

SHERYL CROW
in Ralph Lauren

NATALIE PORTMAN
in Stella McCartney

CLAIRE DANES
in Alexander McQueen

The Emmy Awards

JENNIFER ANISTON
in Chanel

MARISKA HARGITAY
in Vera Wang

AMBER TAMBLYN
in Randolph Duke

JOELY RICHARDSON
in Catherine Walker

HEATHER LOCKLEAR
in Oscar de la Renta

JAMIE-LYNN DISCALA
in Monique Lhuillier

The CFDA
Awards,
New York

The Brit
Awards,
London

The David
di Donatell
Awards,
Rome

SELMA BLAIR
in Isaac Mizrahi

BEYONCE KNOWLES
in Dolce & Gabbana

PENELOPE CRUZ
in Valentino

Shall We Dance? premiere, New York

Raising Helen premiere, Los Angeles

Collateral premiere, London

JENNIFER LOPEZ
in Michael Kors

KATE HUDSON
in Atelier Versace

JADA PINKETT SMITH
in Valentino

The Worst

The Emmys

The Oscars

The Oscars

BARBRA STREISAND

DIANE KEATON

KELLY LYNCH

The Emmys

The Oscars

The Costume Institute Gala

JANE KACZMAREK   UMA THURMAN   ANNE HECHE

Google™

Web Images Groups News Froogle more »

[Unanswered Questions] **Search**

What was the mysterious box-shaped bulge on Bush's back during the first debate?

Faulty tailoring, claims the White House. Foul, cries Bush's tailor, who suggests it was a bulletproof vest. Both wrong, claim bloggers, quoting an unnamed Secret Service agent who says it was a low-frequency "communicator receiver," the President routinely wears. "Anyone can buy one for $150,000," another anonymous source tells the IsBushWired blog, although, he cautions, not "with the same frequency used by the President." Bush's take on the story: "It's just absurd."

Which half of Bennifer really called it off?

It was Affleck who canceled their 2003 wedding four days before the event, citing the attendant media circus, but when they canceled the rematch, a planned wedding at his Georgia estate, it was by mutual consent. After that, the couple continued to see one another, but Ben proved altar shy. "She finally realized they were never going to get married," said a friend of Jen's. In the end, Lopez's rep announced that J.Lo had "ended her engagement to Ben Affleck." But that didn't stop talk that it was really Ben who wanted out and simply left the final say to Jen.

And why isn't J.Lo admitting that she's married to Marc Anthony?

Friends say Lopez keeps mum to discourage an outbreak of a Bennifer-level media blitz. Others think it's because Anthony's signature wasn't dry on his divorce from Dayanara Torres when he wed J.Lo. Either way, the two go to extreme lengths to avoid confirming that they are indeed in a state of wedded bliss, with Anthony ducking direct questions from Matt Lauer, and Jen, though often sporting major wedding bling, coyly asking Diane Sawyer, "What do I know about marriage?"

Was Omarosa Manigault-Stallworth that evil, or was she just hyping it for *The Apprentice?*

"You couldn't melt butter in her mouth," says a fellow contestant. "And her tongue is like a razor blade." Not so, retorts Omarosa's hubby. "She was cast as the villain," Aaron Stallworth says of his wife. In fact, he says, the Washington, D.C., political consultant is "the opposite of what they've chosen to portray on the show. She is constantly laughing, smiling." Or is he being politically correct to keep peace at home?

Did Lindsay Lohan have body-enhancing plastic surgery?

When the *Freaky Friday* and *Mean Girls* teen star began hitting the red carpets in eye- and button-popping dresses that highlighted her stunning new figure, buzz began to circulate that she had gotten implants. "It's retarded," she said shortly before her 18th birthday. "I'm 17 years old. My mother would never let me. I'd be deathly afraid, and it's unnecessary." Even so, allowed Lohan, "I'm glad people think I have a nice chest."

Why isn't Tiger Woods winning anymore?

Some theorists like to paint his Swedish girlfriend turned wife, Elin Nordegren, as golf's incarnation of Yoko Ono or to blame his father Earl's prostate cancer for diverting the linksman's legendary laser focus. Actually, it could be still another relationship at the root of his slump. Woods's failure to win a major tournament since June 2002 coincided with the dismissal of longtime swing instructor Butch Harmon. While urged by advisers to rehire Butchie, the stubborn superstar continued to struggle alone.

What happened to the Hobbits who once lived in the forests of Indonesia?

Fans of Frodo were excited to hear that a group of anthropologists on the Indonesian island of Flores uncovered evidence that a species of three-foot-tall mini-men may have lived as recently as 12,000 years ago. Scientists believe the species was decimated by a volcano, but for centuries local folklore has told of tiny people inhabiting the woodlands, fueling the imagination of geeks everywhere.

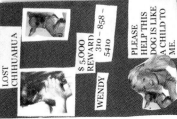

Did Paris Hilton really lose her dog Tinkerbell, or was it a publicity stunt?

The weeklong disappearance of Paris's constant accessory (no, not Nicole Richie) from her Hollywood Hills home coincided curiously with the upcoming release of the unauthorized *Tinkerbell Hilton Diaries*. Adding to the mystery was the initial claim by Hilton family aide Wendy White that the Chihuahua displayed on Missing signs was actually her own mutt let Napoleon. Then she recanted, admitting that the pictured pooch was indeed Tinkerbell, who was returned safely.

Did Paul Hamm deserve his Olympic gold medal?

Despite a miraculous comeback from 12th place in the men's all-around gymnastics final, Hamm faced widespread criticism after officials determined that a scoring error deducted a decisive one-tenth of a point from his South Korean opponent. Tough luck. Hamm refused to return the medal, claiming that he won it fairly. Arbitrators ruled that Hamm should keep the medal, not because he deserved it but because the South Korean's protest was filed too late. This one will be debated for a long time.

Why the devil is *American Idol* reject William Hung so popular?

Barring a pact with the horned one himself, we've got to figure that the tone-deaf Chinese American garnered a few genuine fans because his passion for music overcomes his painful renditions of Top 40 faves. But then again, the American public could just have a mean streak. It's hard not to mockingly embrace an unintentionally hilarious guy with a combination of karaoke-singer-from-hell vocals, klutzy dance moves and awkward wardrobe. While the dorky engineering student may not have been in on the joke, he exploited his cluelessness all the way to the bank.

What really happened between Jay-Z and R. Kelly?

Their Best of Both Worlds tour certainly failed to live up to its billing when a member of rapper Jay-Z's entourage fired a blast of pepper spray at the kinky crooner as he attempted to return to the stage at a concert in Manhattan. Kelly had earlier abruptly left after claiming to see guns in the audience. An angry and disbelieving Jay-Z charged that Kelly "has problems with the love people give me—he's insecure." Whatever the explanation, the fallout resulted in Jay-Z resuming the tour solo and Kelly retaliating with a $75 million suit for breach of contract and sabotage.

THINGS THAT MADE US WANT TO
SCREAM

It was a year of bad and sometimes criminal behavior, poor judgment, foul language and sheer lunacy from the usual suspects and some we thought knew better—and that means you, Mr. Vice President

TRULY OFF THE WALL

In August, two armed, hooded bandits entered Oslo's Munch Museum and—as patrons watched—made off with two works by native son Edvard Munch, including **The Scream**, considered an Expressionist masterpiece of spiritual angst. That was in no short supply among Norwegian officials, excoriated after the heist for laughably poor security at the museum (since closed for renovation). After finding the empty frames nearby, authorities expected a ransom request—the pair were valued at $100 million—but heard only a collective scream from the art world. "Please take care of the paintings," begged museum director Gunnar Srensen of the thieves, "no matter what else you do with them."

TRACEY GOLD
Charged with three felony counts

MACAULAY CULKIN
Faced charges of pot and drug possession

EDWARD FURLONG
Charged with public intoxication

JAMES BROWN
Charged with criminal domestic violence

DON'T YOU KNOW WHO I AM?

There's nothing more humbling, and in many cases more sobering, than a mug shot and fingerprinting session at the local police station. *Growing Pains* actress **Tracey Gold,** 35, faced charges of child endangerment and drunk driving after rolling the family car on a highway near L.A. in September. Her husband, Roby Marshall, was treated for a cervical neck fracture, and two of their three sons suffered minor injuries. That same month another former child star, *Home Alone*'s **Macaulay Culkin,** 24, and a pal were pulled over in Oklahoma during a cross-country car trip. After a vehicle search, cops charged Culkin with possession of pot, sleeping pills and Xanax. Two days earlier, *Terminator 2* star **Edward Furlong,** 27, was arrested for drunkenness after pulling a prank in a supermarket while on location in Kentucky. He was collared for taking live lobsters from a tank and removing the bands from their claws. It was, by contrast, hardly the first time **James Brown,** 71, got himself mugged. Arrested in South Carolina, soul's godfather was charged with criminal domestic violence after his wife, Tomi Rae, 35, was hospitalized with bruises suffered when he pushed her to the ground. "He loves her very much," insisted his lawyer.

It was not a good day in court for **Michael Jackson,** who had just been reprimanded by the judge for arriving 20 minutes late for his arraignment on seven felony counts of lewd or lascivious conduct against a then 12-year-old boy at his Neverland ranch in 2003 and two counts of plying him with an intoxicating agent, believed to be alcohol. Cheered by hundreds of fans as he left the Santa Maria, California, courthouse in January, the once and possibly not future King of Pop acted like it was just another moonwalk in the park. Vaulting on top of his black SUV, he danced on the roof, as his assistants invited a throng of well-wishers for a party back at Neverland. Fort Denial was more like it. The ranch took on a siegelike atmosphere in ensuing months as Jackson, free on $3 million bail since his arrest the previous year, holed up with family members, advisers from the Nation of Islam brought in to help straighten out his affairs, and a legal team that included Scott Peterson's attorney Mark Geragos and a New York City-based lawyer who had defended

Jackson's trial is finally due to begin in early '05. "This may be his last dance," said a friend.

Mob clients like Salvatore "Sammy the Bull" Gravano.

Jackson's parents said they would raise the three kids, Prince Michael I, 7, and II, 2, and Paris Michael, 6, should he lose custody, and his siblings, including sister Janet, formed a united front. Michael, said brother Jermaine, "is 1,000 percent innocent." But cracks began to appear in the spring when Jackson faced yet another charge that he allegedly plotted with coconspirators to abduct his molestation accuser. He threw out his high-priced attorneys and brought in yet another, Thomas Mesereau Jr. (a former Robert Blake defender). This time Jackson, 46, seemed less confident of his case, appearing in court in a sober dark suit and wire-rimmed glasses. "It scared him to death," a friend said of the new indictment. Said another source: "Michael is realizing his own mortality now. He is realizing, 'I could go to prison.'"

SHOOTING FROM THE LIP

Getting caught in the crossfire of these expressive folks is enough to make you say *"Heeeaaaggggh!"*

MEMO TO DAN: CHECK SOURCES

In a kerfuffle dubbed Rathergate, the CBS anchor goofed when he exposed new files questioning President Bush's National Guard service in the '70s. Though their authenticity was doubted by document experts, **Rather**, 73, stuck to his guns, leading observers to suspect his agenda. Six days later, the shaken newsman issued a mea culpa: "It was a mistake. CBS News deeply regrets it. Also, I want to say personally and directly, I'm sorry." In November, Rather announced that he would step down as anchor in 2005 but remain with *60 Minutes*.

Torn got booked for seeming ripped.

This Arizona wildcat in cuffs was Campbell.

Love found herself holed up in a Manhattan jail.

ARRESTING DEVELOPMENT

Famous people get arrested all the time, but it takes something special to make the event infamous. This year's finalists: Although he was later acquitted of drunk driving, the video of a slurring **Rip Torn**, 73, cursing out NYPD cops became a late-night talk show fave. In what sounded like an event in the X Games, **Glen Campbell**, 68, spent 10 nights in a Phoenix jail for "extreme DUI." As for **Courtney Love**, 40, the most chronicled of her two '04 arrests came after she clocked a fan with a mike stand in a New York club, only hours after flashing her breasts at a Wendy's.

YOU SAY TOMATO, SHE SAYS TOMAHTO

As a First Lady contender, the free-spirited **Teresa Heinz Kerry**, 66, was intriguingly different, if not unsettling, to voters accustomed to Laura Bush's more traditionally charming, on-message decorum. The Mozambique-born ketchup heiress never appeared entirely comfortable in the smiling spouse role. At times, like when she pulled 4-year-old Jack Edwards's thumb from his mouth, she turned a routine photo op into a sidebar story that distracted from the Kerry campaign. The nadir occurred in July, when she told a nettlesome reporter from a conservative daily to "shove it." In a CBS interview, Heinz Kerry explained it all in her distinctive accent: "I'm cheeky, I'm sexy, whatever. You know, I've got a lot of life inside."

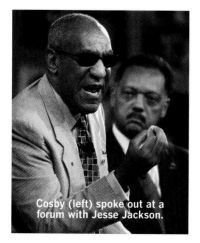

Cosby (left) spoke out at a forum with Jesse Jackson.

COS FOR A CAUSE

Bill Cosby, once a genial Jell-O pitchman, began to push a harder subject with strong rhetoric that stirred controversy in the black community. Too many African-Americans, the sitcom paterfamilias charged, are "not parenting" their kids. "Your dirty laundry," he continued, "gets out of school at 2:30 every day. They can't read, they can't write ... they're going nowhere." Some took offense, dismissing it all as the pompous rant of a millionaire attacking the poor. But NAACP chief Kweisi Mfume said he "agreed with most of what he said." And the now 67-year-old papa continued to preach, organizing town hall meetings in inner cities to discuss ways to attack urban problems.

DO YOU KISS YOUR MOTHER WITH THAT MOUTH?

In not exactly a bipartisan picture of harmony, Vice President **Dick Cheney** told Democratic senator Patrick Leahy to "go [expletive] yourself" during a June photo op on the Senate floor following a testy exchange regarding his continued allegiance to Halliburton. (Cheney had been CEO of the military-contracting monolith prior to becoming veep.) Queried to confirm reports of his vulgar outburst, Cheney stopped just short of a flip-flop, telling Fox News, "That's not the kind of language I usually use. . . . That's not the kind of language I ordinarily use." Further pressed about whether he had, in fact, used the obscenity, the VP sheepishly responded, "Probably." Leahy refused to elaborate but told the *Los Angeles Times*, "I think he was having a bad day."

CAN YOU FEEL THE LOVE TONIGHT?

Not if you were on **Sir Elton John**'s long snit list and among the many he gave a tongue lashing during the year. The temperamental talent seemed especially moody during an outburst in Taiwan, where he cursed out photographers, referring to them as "rude, vile pigs." In fact, the Rocket Man, 57, seemed to be touring behind his anger. Later, he inexplicably cursed his way through a live interview on BBC's Radio 1 and publicly insulted Madonna at a British awards ceremony for lip-synching. "That's me off [Madonna's] Christmas card list," he said. "But do I give a toss? No." As he told an interviewer, "I'm not going to mellow with age. I get more enraged as I get older." The bitch is back.

DEVILISH DIVA

Dubbed "the best reality TV villain of all time" by her *Apprentice* adversary Amy Henry, **Omarosa Manigault-Stallworth**, 30, alienated fellow contenders and many viewers with her frequent embellishments. A shameless self-promoter, the now trademarked Omarosa practically ruined runner-up Kwame's chances by telling fibs and wasting time during the show's final challenge. It got nasty when she made an unsubstantiated claim that rival Ereka Vetrini called her a racial epithet during an argument. Not one to let public perception cloud her dreams, Omarosa set up her own 1-900 line and recently announced ambitions to "be the first female President, thank you very much."

"We're going . . . home."

I HAVE A SCREAM Coming off more like a hog caller than a presidential candidate, former Vermont governor **Howard Dean,** 56, responded to his third-place finish in January's Iowa caucuses with a pumped-up rallying cry punctuated by the soundbite of the year—a wild, high-pitched "*heeeaaaggggh!*" that was replayed hundreds of times in the following days and even inspired dance remixes on the Internet. Once the front-runner, Dean and his anti-Iraq war campaign never recovered from the fallout. "Was it over-the-top? Sure it was over-the-top," Dean later told ABC's Diane Sawyer, one of the few journalists to apologize for the media explosion and overcoverage of his yelp. "But the truth is, I was having a great time."

KEEPING IT

EXTREME MAKEOVER: HOME EDITION

TRADING SPOUSES

"I cry every time I watch," an ABC exec said of the network's hit *Extreme Makeover: Home Edition* (above, with Pennington at far right, and before-and-after shots of a renovated home). In FOX's *Trading Spouses*, the doctor's wife (right, top) came across as a bit bossy, but that was about as bad as it got. The women in this and ABC's counterpart series switched husbands but not bedrooms.

FAMILY MATTERS

Who would have thunk it, but the brazen new trend in reality TV is to celebrate family values and appeal to our better angels. ABC's *Extreme Makeover: Home Edition* actually makes people feel good about themselves and their fellow humans in a way that doesn't involve seeing them humiliated or even embarrassed. In a kind of televised Habitat for Humanity house-raising, the enthusiastic host, rumpled hunk Ty Pennington, leads a winning team of pros who renovate or

demolish and rebuild the homes of needy families. Episodes like one featuring deaf parents and their blind 12-year-old autistic son, and another in which a paralyzed 22-year-old gets an elevator installed in his family's home, lifted ABC's ratings on a flood of tears. As nice-guy carpenter Paul DiMeo says, "It's an emotional show."

Then there's FOX's more scattershot makeover series, *Renovate My Family*, hosted by Jay McGraw, Dr. Phil's equally earnest son. In a combination of *Home Improvement* and

REAL

Once upon a time, romance ruled reality TV. But this year the networks brought it all back home and scored by focusing on family

RENOVATE MY FAMILY

WIFE SWAP

Queer Eye for the Straight Guy, McGraw puts his crew of expert busybodies in the service of troubled households. A garage is turned into a recording studio, a flooded home gets new plumbing, a dad gets a back wax, a mom finally learns how to apply makeup, and a whole family is taught how to argue constructively.

The same two networks also aired dueling mate-switching shows, with FOX scoring a ratings winner with *Trading Spouses.* In the two-part debut, the white wife of an affluent Japanese-American cosmetic surgeon traded

With the Dahm triplets forming a comely construction crew, *Renovate My Family* set out "to help restore and redecorate the lives of families in need," proclaimed FOX. In *Wife Swap,* a pampered New York heiress (top, far left) tried to adjust with a temp husband, while the country mom (bottom, far right) took over child-rearing duties from her big-city counterpart—or rather, from her nannies.

households with a black mother of three. As in ABC's equally successful *Wife Swap,* the titillation was mostly in the title. One of its swaps had a rich Manhattan socialite filling the sturdy shoes of a hardworking rural mom. "I didn't realize," she sighed, "I'd be chopping wood!" In both series, tension was more socioeconomic than sexual. "We're hoping the experience will have some transformational effect on the families," said a *Swap* exec producer. "The last thing that happens is anybody wanting to go to bed with each other."

IT'S IN THE CARDS

Hold 'em or fold 'em, poker was one
of the big reality trends of the year.
Which makes us wonder: What if all
of reality TV was one big poker game?
You know which suit is Trump

THE QUEEN Say what you
want—the critics sure did—about *The
Swan* and its gruesome nip/tuck path to
supposed perfection. Winner **Rachel
Love-Fraser,** 27, will ignore it. "I don't
think anybody should fault anyone for
making themselves a better person,"
said the stepmom, who won the Miss
America-style finale and $50,000. Her
free "improvements," including a nose
job, lip enhancement, liposuction, brow
and breast lifts and chin implant, also
altered her life with husband Michael.
Said Love-Fraser: "We've learned how
much we appreciate one another."

THE ACE With just two little words—"You're fired!"—**Donald
Trump,** 58, electrified his latest venture, and just like his real estate,
The Apprentice is glitzy and over-the-top. (But unlike his casinos
and hair, the series is not in the red.) What makes the boardroom
weekly climax so fraught? All the backstabbing! The hard-boiled
business acumen! The unmasked malevolence! All real, says
Trump, who still looms large despite a second-season dip in ratings.
"I don't consider it acting," he proclaims. "I consider it my life."

THE KING Wait, a nice guy finished first? Okay, technically the burly, bearded **Rupert Boneham,** 40, finished fourth in *Survivor: All Stars.* But when CBS threw the polls open to viewers, more than 8 million of them voted for the Indianapolis youth counselor, given to exuberant hoots and hollers, to win the $1 million Mr. Congeniality consolation prize. That's a lot of tie-dye shirts, plus a new home for him and wife Laura, a college fund for daughter Raya, 5, and $100,000 for a foundation to aid troubled kids. What made the fishing fanatic so popular? Figured Boneham: "I'm that everyday guy people relate to."

JACK & QUEEN OF HEARTS "Boston" Rob **Mariano,** 29, and **Amber Brkich,** 26, did it for love *and* money on *Survivor: All Stars.* During the May finale, Mariano surprised Brkich and 25 million viewers by proposing—just minutes before she won the $1 million purse. (He got $250,000 as runner-up.) The pair will make their alliance permanent next summer. "We're not even a dating show," marveled host Jeff Probst. "Nobody expected this." Adds Brkich: "The fact that Rob proposed before he knew who won just seals it right there for me. This is for real."

THE JOKER The premise had schoolteacher Randi Coy, 24, trying to win $500,000 by duping her parents into thinking she was going to marry a boorish slob and fellow contestant. Gotcha! In *My Big Fat Obnoxious Fiancé,* the joke was on Coy—she'd been punk'd by actor **Steven Bailey,** 33, who belched, drooled and danced in his skivvies all the way to the altar, where he surprised his stunned would-be bride with two checks totaling $1 million and explained to her relieved relatives that it was all just grist for the Nielsens. And for Bailey's career. "My stomach has its own agent now," he deadpanned. "And my butt is getting a lot of calls."

NEW KIDS ON THE BLOCK

These freshmen made quite an impression on us. We lusted after *Desperate Housewives,* got *Lost* in a survival drama, left theaters feeling *Incredible* and learned—finally—how to be a "Redneck Woman"

Former *Party of Five* father figure Matthew Fox leads another orphaned crew through weird circumstances.

LOST The setup gimmick for ABC's *Lost*—a plane crash strands 48 on a remote Pacific isle—sounds like the *Survivor* cast setting sail on the *Minnow.* But creator J.J. Abrams turned it into a whale of a genre-traversing disaster drama, taking about 17 million viewers each week along for the ride.

Abrams, previously the force behind *Felicity* and *Alias,* unleashed sci-fi elements, a polar bear and deadly monsters plus intricate character development, with each episode chronicling what he calls a "hyperreal" day or two in the life. Focused around dashing surgeon Jack Shepard (Matthew Fox), the series also features a druggie has-been rocker (Dominic Monaghan), a wisecracking overweight guy (Jorge Garcia) and an ingenue on the lam from the law (Evangeline Lilly).

Thanks to *Lost* (and *Desperate Housewives*), long-floundering ABC has found itself riding a ratings wave again.

The mischievous ladies of Wisteria Lane (from left): Felicity Huffman, Marcia Cross, Eva Longoria and Teri Hatcher.

DESPERATE HOUSEWIVES In a year when the increasingly supersensitive and censoring FCC got in a huff about the Janet Jackson incident at the Super Bowl, ABC should have known better. Or maybe the network knew exactly what it was doing when it cross-promoted *Desperate Housewives,* its salacious new series, by having a towel-clad Nicolette Sheridan seduce NFL star Terrell Owens during the lead-in to a *Monday Night Football* game. Since its October debut, the deliciously deviant drama had already begun to strike a national nerve, hooking roughly 20 million weekly viewers and voyeurs with its dark humor, retro-cool vibe and exaggerated portrayals of suburban malaise.

A kindred cousin of the long-lost and beloved prime-time soaps of the '80s like *Dynasty* and *Dallas, Desperate Housewives* scored as the season's top new guilty pleasure. "What happened was the networks stopped airing these fun serial dramas," reckoned executive producer Michael Edelstein. "The public just grabbed on." While their Anytown, U.S.A., locale of Wisteria Lane seemed transplanted from the set of *Leave It to Beaver,* the show focused on four neighborhood pals who have trampled their inner Cleaver. Lynette (Felicity Huffman) is a business exec turned stay-at-home mom, Susan (Teri Hatcher) a sweetly neurotic single mom, Gabrielle (Eva Longoria) a former model, and Bree (Marcia Cross) a tightly wound homemaker.

Besides giving ABC a much-needed hit, the show has provided a midlife career revival for series veterans like Hatcher, 40, Cross, 42, Huffman, 42, and Nicolette Sheridan, 41, who plays the sexually ravenous divorcée Edie. "It's really nice doing this at this point in my life," said the former *Knots Landing* star. Hatcher, who had lately been hawking Radio Shack, was equally grateful for ABC's new Sex and the Suburbs. "Two years ago," she said, "I'm crying on my kitchen floor thinking I'll never be able to pay my mortgage."

DEADWOOD Howdy, pardner? More like howdy, @#%*!*. HBO's gritty Wild West drama was certainly one of the most profane shows ever to hit the tube. It also had a posse of critics swearing that it was one of the best—period—winning two Emmys in its first season. Mixing dark comedy with grim violence (like its lead-in *The Sopranos*), *Deadwood* told the story of an unauthorized settlement in the Black Hills of South Dakota in 1876 and its unique system of frontier justice. The lawless locale was a prime destination for an interesting array of gold grubbers, and town bully Al Swearengen (Ian McShane) was there to provide them with booze, women and choice quips like "I woulda let him lay in state, but I needed the room for my whores." Incorporating real-life gunslinger Wild Bill Hickok (Keith Carradine) into the cast with a token businessman of conscience (Timothy Olyphant), the series managed to appeal to western fans who wanted the good and bad with their ugly. And the unexpected. In the words of Swearengen: "Announcing your plans is a good way to hear God laugh."

This ain't network TV, bucko: Though Carradine was one of the show's stars, his character was killed off in the premiere season.

THE O.C.
Although the Southern California spectacle premiered the previous summer, it wasn't until '04 that the melodramedy caught the perfect wave. This generation's *90210,* albeit with an ironic sense of humor and self-deprecating dialogue, *The O.C.* has inspired great catchphrases ("Eeew" and "Chrismukkah" among them), a whole new brood of sex symbols (including Mischa Barton and Benjamin McKenzie) and a rabidly devoted fan base. Whether obsessing over the real-life romance of onscreen couple Adam Brody and Rachel Bilson or playing along to the *O.C.* drinking game, viewers of all ages have become intoxicated with the show. That may give *O.C.* writers license to reduce the swimming pool brawls that juiced up the show's inaugural year. "I am going to get into fewer fistfights," said McKenzie about the development of brooding bad boy Ryan. "We have to prove we weren't a fluke."

Welcome back to *The O.C.* (clockwise from top left): Tate Donovan, Bilson, Melinda Clarke, Peter Gallagher, Kelly Rowan, Chris Carmack, Brody, McKenzie and Barton.

Clockwise from top: "Redneck Woman" Wilson; red-hot L.A. quintet Maroon 5; double platinum-selling producer/rapper West; and the Scottish rockers dubbed for a dead Austrian, Franz Ferdinand.

MUSICIANS When tough-livin' country singer Gretchen Wilson bested rap wunderkind Kanye West to win Best New Artist at the American Music Awards, the choice wasn't unanimous. "*I* was the best new artist this year," challenged West, who threatened to boycott the show in the future. But West had a point: When it came to breakthrough artists this year, the level of competition was high. Our nominations for rookies of the year:

Kanye West The 27-year-old producer turned rapper, who grew up in Chicago, didn't need to fake a gangsta rep to sell nearly 3 million copies of his debut *The College Dropout.* He won fans with a mix of old-school production techniques and soul-searching, confessional lyrics.

Gretchen Wilson The ex-bartender, 31, is a tobacco-chewin', Illinois-bred throwback to the rough-and-tumble days of country music. Her hit single "Redneck Woman" debuted at No. 2 on the *Billboard* pop charts by celebrating double-wide pride with lines like "I ain't no high-class broad . . ./ I say, 'hey y'all,' and 'yee-haw.'"

Franz Ferdinand Massively hyped in Britain before signing a million-dollar deal with Epic, the Glasgow quartet made a splash on U.S. alternative radio with the single "Take Me Out." Named after the assassinated Austrian archduke, the hipster faves blended a mix of '70s art rock and '80s new wave to create the catchy sounds of their self-titled major-label debut.

Maroon 5 The road to stardom was pokier for the soulful pop rockers from Southern California. It took nearly two years for the band's *Songs About Jane* to crack the Top 10. Along the way, they built buzz and pushed their single "Harder to Breathe," opening for artists like John Mayer and Sheryl Crow. Says singer Adam Levine, 25: "We're trying not to let it get to our heads."

ARRESTED DEVELOPMENT Although the quirky comedy finished its first season a dismal 107th in the Nielsens, the few viewers included, fortunately, a clued-in quorum of Emmy voters. The ensemble production about the wildly dysfunctional Bluth real estate clan took home trophies for comedy series, directing for a comedy series, and writing for a comedy series at the awards ceremony in September. One of the rare sitcoms confident enough to fly without a laugh track, *Arrested Development* ventures bizarre plots (in one episode, the family's drunken mother accidentally adopts a Korean boy) and wicked humor that not everybody would love like, say, *Raymond*. Most of the TV reviewers did get behind it, and so, at the start of the second season, did FOX, putting the show in a slot where it might hook a simpatico audience—immediately following *The Simpsons*.

Imprisoned patriarch George (Jeffrey Tambor) and son Michael (Jason Bateman) are just two of the show's irreverent characters.

It's better to be exceptional, said *The Incredibles*, than average. Some thought the message was too red-state, but audiences put the movie in the black.

THE INCREDIBLES A computer-generated family of five do-gooders in tights, The Incredibles proved as compelling and charming as Superman or Spidey in their cinematic prime. Incorporating a sophisticated mix of comedy and character development, they wowed audiences of all ages and could outgross any film in Pixar studio history, including earlier classics *Toy Story* and *Finding Nemo*. The imaginative tale featured Mr. Incredible (voiced by Craig T. Nelson) and his wife, Elastigirl (Holly Hunter), who, forced into early retirement (because they'd generated too many costly nuisance lawsuits), slunk off to suburbia with their three offspring. The superannuated superhero toils at an insurance company, leading his bored spouse to wryly encourage him to "Go save the world, one policy at a time." Fortunately, a villainous archenemy (Jason Lee) sets out to destroy the world, and the Incredible family redon their capes and swing back into action. A few reviewers claimed that the film's story lines showed a conservative bias. Most disagreed, and by year's end *The Incredibles* was being talked up by some critics for a Best Picture Oscar.

A staggering 52.5 million misty-eyed viewers caught the show's heartstring-tugging finale.

THAT'S A WRAP

THE TOP 10 REASONS WE'RE GOING TO MISS...

1. WHAT'S TO TALK ABOUT FRIDAY MORNING? From the pilot episode, when Rachel burst into Central Perk in a wedding dress after leaving her groom standing at the altar, until the last, when she and Ross finally hooked up, again, their romantic misadventures, as well as those of Monica and Phoebe and Joey and Chandler, fueled a decade's worth of hot watercooler chat.

2. NOW NO ONE IN PRIME TIME IS MARRIED TO BRAD PITT The real-life loves and losses of stars Jennifer Aniston, Courteney Cox, David Schwimmer, Matthew Perry, Lisa Kudrow and Matt LeBlanc were as gossip-worthy as their fictional counterparts'.

3. NOW WE'LL NEVER KNOW HOW PACINO FELT ABOUT IT "After all your years of struggling, you've finally been able to crack your way into show business," Chandler said when Joey announced he'd landed a part as Al Pacino's "butt double."

4. THERE'S NO OPEN-MIKE NIGHT ON MTV Phoebe achieved singer-songwriter immortality with her Central Perk rendition of "Smelly Cat."

5. SELF-HELP BOOKS AREN'T AS FUNNY When whippet-thin Cox donned her "fat Monica" prosthesis to dance with her teenage self, supersize fans took heart.

6. NEITHER IS O. HENRY With echoes of *Gift of the Magi,* Chandler, harboring a crush on Joey's girlfriend (played by Paget Brewster), allowed his rival to give her the touching gift he picked out for her.

7. NOR IS YOUR TYPICAL FIRST-AID MANUAL When Monica was stung by a jellyfish at the beach, Chandler soothed the pain by urinating on the wound.

8. UNTIL *FRIENDS*, WE ALWAYS THOUGHT TV CASTS WERE JUST ACTING Any doubts that they were pals off-camera were dispelled by the May 6 sign-off, when, Perry said, all six shared "a huge sadness that the experience of our lifetime was coming to a close."

9. WE NEVER GOT THE ANSWER The girls lost their apartment in a bet when they failed to answer the trivia question "What is Chandler Bing's job?"

10. NOW *SURVIVOR* IS THE ONLY TV REFUGE FOR UGLY NAKED GUYS In the first episode of the first season, the rear-window running gag was introduced with Chandler's immortal words: "Ew! Ew! Ew! Ew! Ugly Naked Guy got a ThighMaster!"

FRIENDS

"I think I'll go home and rearrange my sock drawer," Brokaw, 64, said of his retirement plans.

THE TOP 5 REASONS WE'RE GOING TO MISS...

1. HE'S NOT JUST A PRETTY FACE Though said to be the model for William Hurt's pretty-boy anchor in *Broadcast News,* Brokaw was a seasoned reporter who was happiest covering stories from the White House to the collapse of the Berlin Wall.

2. HE CAN ACTUALLY WRITE While serving as anchor and managing editor of *NBC Nightly News* (for 21 years) and cohost of *Dateline NBC,* Brokaw found time to write four well-regarded historical books, most memorably *The Greatest Generation,* about American soldiers who served in World War II.

3. HE'S A DOWN-HOME BOY Under those tailored suits, the Webster, South Dakota, native sported hand-tooled cowboy boots.

TOM BROKAW

4. HE HAS A LIFE Married since 1962 and the father of three daughters, he spends his spare time fly-fishing, bird hunting and mountain climbing.

5. HE KNOWS THE FREQUENCY While he admires his longtime CBS rival, he spared us Dan Rather's hokey metaphorical reaches. Where Rather reckoned that the recent presidential race was tight enough to give aspirin a headache, Brokaw saw it as "a story of almost Shakespearean proportion."

In terms of finales and farewells, this was a year to remember. With the sign-off of *Friends, Frasier, Sex and the City* and two trusted news anchors, our TV lives will never be the same, and here's why

By the end of their six-season run, Nixon (left), Parker, Davis and Cattrall had become pop-culture icons.

FRASIER

1. WE HATE THE WORDS "LAST CALL" As radio shrink Frasier Crane (Kelsey Grammer) signed off in Seattle, he was shutting the tap on a character who was our last link with the late, lamented *Cheers,* where Frasier began life in 1984 as a pompous barfly. The only prime-time figure with a comparable run was *Gunsmoke*'s Marshall Matt Dillon (James Arness).

2. NOW THE EMMYS ARE TOUGHER TO PREDICT *Frasier* scooped up five consecutive Emmy awards for outstanding comedy. Not a bad batting average for an 11-season series.

3. NO MORE EDDIE! At the last taping, *Frasier*'s cast and crew cheered Moose, the now 14-year-old Jack Russell terrier who first played Eddie (his son Enzo later replaced him). "Moose is pretty old and pretty heavy, snow white and stone deaf," said David Hyde Pierce (Niles). "But he knows when people are applauding."

4. JACK BENNY JUNKIES NEED A FIX Not since the late, great Jack Benny have TV viewers been treated to such a perfect, self-deprecating, deadpan double take as Kelsey Grammer's.

5. EFFETE SNOBS HAVE LOST A ROLE MODEL Of course, there's always *Will & Grace,* but that's a slightly different story.

"There was a lot of crying," Grammer said of taping the final episode of *Frasier.* "But also a lot of laughing."

SEX AND THE CITY

1. WE'LL NO LONGER HAVE A CLUE ABOUT JIMMY CHOO "The show liberated the way women felt they could dress," designer Patricia Field said about the influence of Miranda (Cynthia Nixon), Carrie (Sarah Jessica Parker), Charlotte (Kristin Davis) and Samantha (Kim Cattrall) on fashion. "They could be more eclectic, show more skin."
2. NOW NEW YORK IS JUST ANOTHER GRITTY STOMPING GROUND FOR COP AND TALK SHOWS From horse-drawn-carriage rides in Central Park to life-affirming swings on a flying trapeze, *Sex* cast the city in its most romantic light since the early Woody Allen.
3. MEETING CUTE WAS NEVER SO NAUGHTY Carrie found the love of her televised life, Mr. Big (Chris Noth), when he gallantly stooped in the street to pick up what had tumbled from her purse: condoms.
4. IN MOST SHOWS, A GUY THAT GOOD-LOOKING IS ALWAYS A CREEP When waiter-turned-actor Smith Jerrod (Jason Lewis) shaved his gorgeous head in sympathy with Samantha's cancer-bared scalp, she sensed the younger man might be her long-elusive One.
5. LIFE WITHOUT *SEX* IS DREARY Forced to abstain from *Sex* while *The Sopranos* and *Six Feet Under* are both on long breaks between seasons, viewers find the ads are wrong—HBO is plain old TV after all.

THE LATE LATE SHOW WITH CRAIG KILBORN

He and guest Will Ferrell stayed up *Late Late.*

1. HE DIDN'T SUFFER FROM SELF-DOUBT When announcing that he was abandoning his *Late Late Show* after five seasons of pummeling from time-slot competitor Conan O'Brien, Kilborn said, "I felt like I did all I could do for that particular show."
2. HE WAS EASY ON THE EYE The single guy was once rated "sexiest late-night talk show host" in a survey, outpolling Ted Koppel (!) by one percentage point.
3. HE DANCED TO HIS OWN MUSIC In lieu of a house band, Kilborn booked a range of musical guests from Uncle Kracker to Morrissey, who took up a weeklong residence.
4. HE WAS THE GREAT WASP HOPE Though the whitest of white men, he longed to jump, once joining in a team scrimmage with the Minnesota Timberwolves. When outgunned, he reminded the 'Wolves, "Guys, I'm 41!"
5. HE COULD TAKE A JOKE "Are you daring people to beat you up?" an interviewer asked of his referring to himself as "Kilby" and "Craiggers." "It's a bit of moxie," he replied.

BARBARA WALTERS

1. WE CAN'T BELIEVE WHAT SHE PUT UP WITH Breaking into the man's world that was NBC *Today* in 1961, the future *20/20* host had to apprentice as a writer. When she did get on-camera, she was told not to ask questions about topics like economics and politics.
2. TED KOPPEL NEVER ASKED WHAT KIND OF TREE YOU WANT TO BE Unpredictable queries made for riveting TV, as when she asked Katharine Hepburn to share her secret arboreal fantasies.
3. WE CHEER FOR TEARS Her knack for eliciting emotional responses from subjects led critics to slag her for practicing non-serious journalism, but viewers gave her ratings Koppel would kill for.
4. WE'RE HUGE GILDA RADNER FANS A Boston-born club owner's daughter, Walters developed a highly imitatable style that inspired *Saturday Night Live* parodists from Radner to Cheri Oteri.
5. SHE HAS GREAT REFERENCES As the first woman network news anchor (she landed the ABC Evening News slot in 1976), she is listed in the *American Heritage Dictionary*.

In her four decades in the business, Walters, 75, compiled an incomparable reel, including the 1999 Monica Lewinsky "get" that was the most-watched journalistic interview ever.

TRIBUTES

We fondly remember the Great Communicator, acting godfather Marlon Brando, soul genius Ray Charles and the saucy servings of Julia Child—and pay respects to many other lost favorites, including, yes, Rodney Dangerfield

> *"What I'd really like to do is go down in history as the President who made Americans believe in themselves again"*

RONALD REAGAN

Born 1911 Could he do that? Could he call the Soviet Union an "evil empire"? Didn't he check with focus groups first? How about bombing Libya because the country had killed a U.S. serviceman in a terrorist attack in Berlin? Didn't he need U.N. permission? And firing 11,000 air traffic controllers for breaking the law and walking off their jobs? How would that play in the swing states?

But Ronald Reagan did all this, and many more controversial things, in defiance of those who counseled caution. Caution, it's safe to say, was not his strong suit.

Reagan was a man who acted, in both senses of the word. The guy who played second banana to a chimp in his Hollywood years became the world's leading man. When the moment required a brilliant one-liner, he always had one at the ready; to an attack by then President Jimmy Carter

Son Ron, Rev. Michael Wenning, wife Nancy and daughter Patti paused for a private moment of reflection prior to the public viewing period at the Ronald Reagan Presidential Library in Simi Valley, California.

The new First Couple celebrated a high point in their 52-year marriage at the Inaugural Ball in 1981. "My life really began with Ronnie," said Nancy.

at a 1980 debate, it was "There you go again." When shot by John Hinckley Jr. outside the Washington Hilton barely two months into his first term in 1981, he told his wife, Nancy, "Honey, I forgot to duck." (His wit may have been intact, but he lost more than half his blood supply; the bullet missed his heart by one inch.) Upon regaining consciousness after surgery, he scribbled on a piece of paper, "I'd like to do this scene again." And most famously, he stood at the Berlin Wall in 1987 to bellow, "Mr. Gorbachev, tear down this wall!" Only slightly off cue, the wall burst open two years later.

To his critics, the roles he declined are also part of the Reagan record. His refusal to address both the massive social epidemics of AIDS and homelessness clearly contrasted with his image as the genial, compassionate optimist. The creation of a presidential AIDS commission (without a gay representative or sufficient budget) and pushing an emergency care bill for the homeless in 1987 were widely viewed as mere lip service. And the Iran-Contra scandal seemed like the first draft of a spy farce. It was never proven, though,

Reagan was a man who acted, in both senses of the word. The guy who played second banana to a chimp in his Hollywood years became the world's leading man

that Reagan okayed negotiating for the release of American hostages in Lebanon by selling arms to Iran and then using some of the proceeds to fund the Communist-fighting Contras in Nicaragua.

Throughout it all, his costar Nancy was at his side, from their marriage in 1952 through the 10-year battle with terminal Alzheimer's that he announced in a poignant handwritten open letter to the world. At the end, Nancy was joined at his bedside by their two children Patti and Ron as well as his son Michael from his marriage to actress Jane Wyman. On their first date in Hollywood, where Nancy Davis was an actress and Reagan, already the president of the Screen Actors Guild, was hobbling on crutches because he had broken his leg in a charity baseball game, they put away two bottles of champagne and stayed out till 3 a.m. "When the real thing comes along," she later wrote about that evening, "you just know it."

Reagan was 49 and Nancy 39 when they showed off Ron, 2, and Patti, 7, in Pacific Palisades in 1960. The once-estranged kids returned to the fold during Dad's illness.

REAGAN'S GREATEST LINES

"They prepared for their journey and waved goodbye and slipped the surly bonds of Earth to touch the face of God."
Following the spaceship Challenger *disaster, 1986*

"Are you better off than you were four years ago?"
During the debate versus President Jimmy Carter, 1980

"Win one for the Gipper."
Playing George Gipp in Knute Rockne— All American, *1940*

"Please tell me you're Republicans."
To surgeons while entering the hospital following the assassination attempt, 1981

"I now begin the journey that will lead me into the sunset of my life. I know that for America there will always be a bright dawn ahead."
From his letter declaring he suffered from Alzheimer's, 1994

The running mates in his 50-plus movies included Virginia Mayo in *The Girl from Jones Beach* (1949) and a mischievous chimp in *Bedtime for Bonzo* (1951). Serving as president of the Screen Actors Guild, he said, "I first tasted politics."

CHRISTOPHER REEVE Born 1952

After four crowd-pleasing flights as Superman, it was time, he said, to "escape the cape." But he did so in a way no one could have envisioned or wished. Tragedy transformed the actor into a true crusader and real-life hero whose undaunted spirit moved and inspired the world. "He showed us," said Steven Spielberg, "that through courage, tenacity, generosity and faith we can all be Superman." With knowing humor and an endearing, self-deprecating charm, he turned the iconic action

"Theirs was a love affair," Barbara Walters said of the Reeves. A tragedy, said Dana, "can either tear you away or make [the relationship] stronger. It made us stronger."

"If it hadn't happened," he told Jane Seymour post-paralysis, people would have said of him, "'Oh, he's that actor who used to do that thing with a cape.'"

hero and his bumbling alter ego Clark Kent into multidimensional characters, boosting 1978's *Superman: The Movie* to what was then the biggest box office opening ever. Astonishing good looks and a buff, 6'4" athletic frame didn't hurt. Reeve was a hunk with a heart offscreen as well. A skilled sailor and pilot, he twice did the Lindy Hop across the pond, flying planes solo over the Atlantic. A political activist, he campaigned for liberal causes and flew to Chile to protest the Pinochet dictatorship's threatened execution of 77 activist actors.

Somehow he also found time to ski, scuba dive and compete in equestrian events like the one in Virginia in 1995, in which his Thoroughbred balked at a jump, leaving Reeve paralyzed with two fractured cervical ver-

"I'm not leading the life I thought I would, but it does have meaning. There is love, there is joy, there is laughter"

tebrae. When he considered suicide, his family pulled him back from the abyss. "You're still you, and I love you" were his wife Dana's life-saving words. Enduring endlessly painful physical therapies in hopes of regaining control over his body, one tremulous flick of a finger at a time, he lobbied Congress and medical science for stem-cell research and insurance reform to benefit others suffering catastrophic illness and injuries. Buoyed by his family (he had two children by a previous relationship as well as his son Will, 12, with Dana), he continued to act and direct. "There were obvious physical limitations," said a colleague he directed recently, "but there were no creative limitations." "Chris had far greater challenges than I've faced," said his friend Michael J. Fox, following Reeve's sudden death from a severe infection. "And he faced them with a courage, intelligence and dignity I can only aspire to."

A HERO'S WORDS OF INSPIRATION

"I've just decided I won't listen to the rules. I mean, how many people are walking around who have been told by a doctor [they've] got six months to live? It's just a hell of a lot harder than I'd thought it was going to be—but that's no excuse. You just have to keep going."

"I get pretty impatient with people who are able-bodied but are somehow paralyzed for other reasons."

"For everyone who thought I couldn't do it. For everyone who thought I shouldn't do it. For everyone who said, 'It's impossible.' See you at the finish line!" —*a sign in Reeve's workout room*

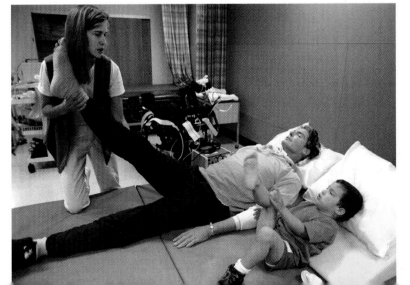

Will (joining Mom and Dad in a therapy session) was 2 when the accident happened. Reeve helped him learn to bike through verbal coaching and attended his sporting events, including a hockey game the night before he died.

"Music to me is like breathing. I have to have it. It's a part of me, just like my liver or my kidney is a part of me"

RAY CHARLES

Born 1930 Thank God for Tab Hunter. If the pop pinup hadn't lifted Ray Charles's arrangement of "I Can't Stop Loving You" and released his own sanitized, soulless cover, Charles might never have transformed American popular music. His original "Can't Stop"—at the time just a cut on his yet-to-be-released 1962 album *Modern Sounds in Country and Western Music*—was rushed to radio stations as a result, and deejays soon spun the real thing (not the Tab) into gold. The single sold millions and topped the pop, country and rhythm & blues charts—matching a trifecta achieved only by Elvis Presley. In the process, *Modern Sounds* was also propelled to No. 1 and became one of the great pop-world-shaking classics of all time. Most (read: white) Americans didn't know what soul music was until they heard it roll forth from Brother Ray's majestic tears-and-blues-steeped voice. For black listeners who long endured what they saw as the exploitation and, often, emasculation of their music, this was payback time. And by rediscovering the soul of the southern workingman's blues, said Willie Nelson, "Ray Charles did more for country music than any other artist."

This from a blind black man born to lose in the segregated South that spawned both the blues and what Charles called, simply, "hillbilly." The pain he knew went far beyond the dues demanded of all who sing the blues. His father bolted soon after his birth, and his mother's death left him an orphan at 15. Tragedy struck years earlier. When he was 5, he stood shocked and helpless as his little brother drowned in a steel washtub. Two year later he lost his sight after his glaucoma went untreated because hospitals were closed to blacks in those Jim Crow days in Florida, where

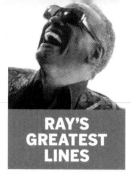

RAY'S GREATEST LINES

"Hey mama don't you treat me wrong/ Come and love your daddy all night long"
"What'd I Say," 1959

"Woah, woman, oh woman, don't treat me so mean/ You're the meanest old woman that I've ever seen/ I guess if you say so/ I'll have to pack my things and go (That's right)"
"Hit the Road, Jack," 1961

"I'm broke, no bread, I mean like nothing"
"Busted," 1963

"Oh, it's cryin' time again, you're gonna leave me/ I can see that faraway look in your eyes"
"Crying Time," 1966

"My mom would say, 'You might not be able to do things like a person who can see,'" said Charles (in 1960). "'You've just got to find the other way.'"

he grew up. But Ray Charles Robinson—he dropped the surname when he launched his professional career to avoid confusion with boxing great Sugar Ray Robinson—refused to become traumatized or bitter; nor did he bow to poverty or the limitations of his handicap. "Times and me got leaner and leaner," he said. "But anything beats getting a cane and a cup and picking out a street corner."

From a life sown in sorrow and hatred, Charles created a music that enriched the world. He called his style "pure heart singing." And his indeed was a voice of undiluted feeling, spring-fed by the soul. It was an instrument both joyous and pain-drenched. It was resonant and rich in harmony and humor. It was uplifting, and it was knowingly carnal. "What'd I Say," then one of the most suggestive aural acts ever committed on mainstream radio, was banned from many playlists in 1959. That song and others, like "I've Got a Woman" and "Unchain My Heart," earned Charles his "Genius of Soul" tag. He is credited with creating the fusion of gospel's rhythmic and vocal styles with the salacious lyrics of the blues. High whoops and low bedroom moans were substituted for the spiritual's more heavenly trills. "All I was doing was being myself," he said. "I sing what I feel, what I genuinely feel. That's it. No airs."

Ray Charles will be remembered not for his lack of sight but for his spirit-stirring sounds. "Hearing," he declared, "is the most important thing in the world." And his Ray Charles Foundation today aids not the blind but the deaf. Twice divorced and the father of a dozen children (and granddad of 20), Charles died in his Beverly Hills home of liver disease. For friends like B.B. King, who broke down onstage, and Nelson, who sang a sob-inducing rendition of "Georgia on My Mind" at his funeral, it felt like music's heart had given out.

"Heaven has become a much better place with him in it," said Quincy Jones (in 1970). Lifelong friends, they met as teenage music prodigies in Seattle.

Charles (with Janet Jackson in 2002, at right) bridged genres and eras from *The Blues Brothers* (with Dan Aykroyd and John Belushi in 1980, far left) to the D.C. Kennedy Center, where he was honored along with Lucille Ball and Hume Cronyn in 1986. "I never considered myself part of rock and roll," he said. "My stuff was more adult."

"Even today," Brando said years after *Streetcar*, "I meet people who think of me automatically as a tough, insensitive, coarse guy. They can't help it, but it is troubling."

*In The Wild One,
"there's a line where Johnny
snarls, 'Nobody tells me
what to do.' That's exactly how
I've felt all my life"*

MARLON BRANDO

Born 1924 Countless Method men, from James Dean to Johnny Depp, followed in his shadow. Before him, there had been no one quite like Marlon Brando. He was the actor from another planet. Like Elvis Presley, who came a few years later, Brando set the culture on its ear performing an ancient art in a startling new way. Where old-school actors played their parts, Brando stormed to life in them. His mumble was a roar. He was unsettling to behold. Audiences didn't merely watch him work—they braced for trouble. So did costars. "You never know what he's going to do next, where he's going or what he's going to say," said Vivien Leigh, his costar in *A Streetcar Named Desire,* the film that turned his torn and grimy T-shirts into fetish items and made the world mad for the man and his Method. Brando's Stanley Kowalski was an emotional predator; but for all the allure and danger of his stalking sexuality, the anguish in his voice when he cried *"Stel-laaah!"* was the essence of human frailty. His performance struck Hollywood like a brush fire, and the actor himself seemed caught in the flames. Stanley, Brando once said, was "aggres-

Before his trial for the death of his sister's boyfriend, Christian (center) was joined by his dad and brother Miko. Christian served nearly five years.

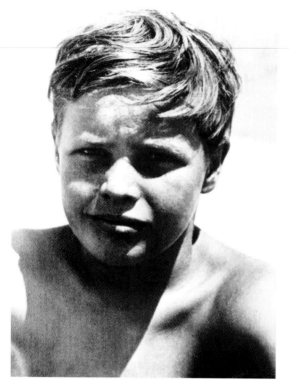

"Bud" to his family, the rebellious boy (here at 10) was banished to military school by Marlon Sr.

sive and completely without doubt about himself." In fact, he continued, the character was "the direct antithesis of what I am."

Brando inhabited a tortured emotional landscape that he tapped for his art but masked behind a combative public persona. Glimpses were offered in the X-rated *Last Tango in Paris,* his most searingly personal performance, and in his 1994 autobiography *Songs My Mother Taught Me.* Both his parents were alcoholics whose self-indulgences traumatized him, he wrote. He loved his mother, herself a frustrated actor, but, he added with devastating bluntness, she "ignored me." Of his namesake father, an Omaha-based traveling salesman, Brando wrote that he "tortured me emotionally and made my mother's life a misery."

His life as a teen (he was booted out of high school for driving a motorcycle through the halls) imitated his future art. "What are you rebelling against, Johnny?" Brando's biker gang leader is asked in *The Wild One,* the 1954 angst-ploitation movie that would spark a run on leather jackets and dormitory wall posters. "Whaddaya got?" was his reply.

For Brando, acting offered a way to slip out of his own painful skin. "I have been looking for a way to repair myself," he once said. A few fixes took. He was one of the first to march with Martin Luther King Jr., and he long crusaded for

Brando and Tahitian third wife Tarita Teriipaia (with son Simon) co-starred in *Mutiny on the Bounty.*

Native American rights. But he never passed up an opportunity to tweak the industry. At the 1973 Academy Awards ceremony, he memorably dispatched actress Maria Cruz (posing as the fancifully named Indian princess Sacheen Littlefeather) to decline his Best Actor Oscar for *The Godfather*. The statuette she refused was his second trophy—out of an ultimate eight nominations—and marked a mid-career revival after a long mutual boycott.

Brando had at least 11 children in and out of three marriages, but no romantic relationship was lasting. In the wake of his son Christian's 1991 manslaughter trial and his troubled daughter Cheyenne's 1995 suicide, Brando no longer visited his beloved Tahitian island and seldom ventured out in public. He seemed to retreat behind the walls of his Beverly Hills home within the great mountain of flesh that girthed a once gorgeous, muscular star. "When I wanted to feel better or had a crisis," he said, "I'd open the icebox."

Sir Laurence Olivier called him America's finest actor; to film critic Pauline Kael, he was "the greatest" of our time

Reviewers and fans regretted that he wasted his talent on bizarre absurdities like *The Island of Dr. Moreau* or on empty but high-paying roles like Superman's father. The drummer's son never left us a Brando version of *Death of a Salesman*. In the end, he was a broken-down colossus, dependent on an oxygen tank when his lungs failed. But his legacy was clear. "There was no way to follow in his footsteps," said Jack Nicholson. "He truly shook the world."

In A Streetcar Named Desire

MARLON'S MEMORABLE LINES

"You was my brother, Charley, you shoulda looked out for me a little bit. . . . I coulda had class, I coulda been a contender. I coulda been somebody, instead of a bum, which is what I am, let's face it."
On the Waterfront, 1954

"How 'bout cuttin' the re-bop."
A Streetcar Named Desire, 1951

"I'm gonna make him an offer he can't refuse."
The Godfather, 1972

"The horror. The horror."
Apocalypse Now, 1979

The Godfather

The Wild One

Apocalypse Now

Last Tango in Paris

Playfully with Larry King in 1994, Brando regarded his own celebrity as meaningless buffoonery.

TUG McGRAW, 59 A cool, quotable relief pitcher, he died at the Tennessee home of his country-music star son Tim.

ALEXANDRA RIPLEY, 70 She created a literary storm with *Scarlett,* her 1991 "sequel" to *Gone with the Wind.*

UTA HAGEN, 84 The revered drama coach and Broadway actress won a Tony in 1963 for *Who's Afraid of Virginia Woolf?*

OLIVIA GOLDSMITH, 54 Her barbed comic novel *The First Wives Club* became a hit film. Her death followed complications from cosmetic surgery.

LLOYD BUCHER, 76 The skipper of the ill-fated USS *Pueblo,* captured by North Korea in 1968, endured 11 months of brutal imprisonment.

JAN MINER, 86 The actress played Madge, the wise-cracking manicurist, in Palmolive commercials for 27 years.

MERCEDES McCAMBRIDGE, 87 The 1950 Oscar winner (*All the King's Men*) gave voice to the demon possessing Linda Blair in *The Exorcist.*

"Comedy," said King, "is a distorted mirror in the fun house. You're laughing at yourself."

ALAN KING Born 1927 An actor as well as a stand-up comic, Alan King once played God on an episode of *Murphy Brown* and was frequently cast as His second banana, a rabbi. "Modesty is not one of my virtues," he said. Nor decorum. When Queen Elizabeth greeted him with "How do you do, Mr. King?" at a formal reception, he responded, "How do you do, Mrs. Queen?" Brooklyn-born, he trouped New York's so-called Borscht Belt as a teen and wound up under the wing of Milton Berle. King's later humor was mined from his suburban New York lifestyle. A dad of three, he had been married 57 years when he died of lung cancer. To pal Jerry Stiller, King was "a Jewish Will Rogers. He was in touch with the world, which is what made him so funny."

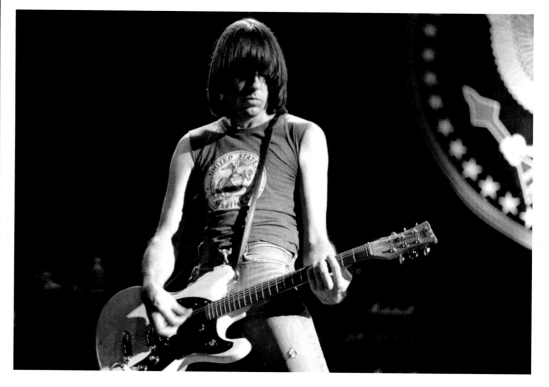

"I wanted our sound to be original," he said. "I stopped listening to everything [else]."

JOHNNY RAMONE Born 1948 The look, like the sound, was unwavering. With his legs wide spread, his guitar low slung, his facial expression hangdog, his hair in a bowl cut, his jeans ripped and his sneakers black, he played his blitzkrieg guitar licks at maximum volume. Along with his three (unrelated) fellow Ramones from Queens, Johnny (né John Cummings) helped invent punk rock, limning intense two-minute anthems bristling with humor and hooks. Though bands they inspired, from the Sex Pistols to Green Day, harvested riches and glory, the Ramones (their fictional surname came from an alias Paul McCartney used checking into hotels) never scored a hit in 22 years. Johnny, who died of cancer, joining Joey and Dee Dee in punk paradise, was philosophic about the band's belated induction into the Rock and Roll Hall of Fame: "Better late than never."

Child "demystified French cuisine in an appealing, straightforward way," said Jacques Pepin, her longtime PBS partner.

JULIA CHILD
Born 1912 Without her, the Food Network would be roller derby. After serving in World War II with the OSS in Ceylon (now the CIA and Sri Lanka), Child picked up a whisk and launched a French revolution in American kitchens. With common sense and breezy bonhomie, the coauthor of the monumental *Mastering the Art of French Cooking* strode, all 6'2" of her, onto PBS in 1963 as *The French Chef* and stayed for most of four decades. A stickler for technique, she nonetheless shrugged off fallen soufflés and would simply scrape mishaps back into the pan. "You're alone in the kitchen, no one will see you," she counseled conspiratorially in her much-parodied foghorn falsetto. Her recipe for the good life—spent primarily in Cambridge, Massachusetts, with her husband of 48 years, Paul—included dollops of ebullience and butter and especially, she said, "red meat and gin." She died from kidney failure two days shy of 92. As she ended each episode, a cheery "Bon appétit!"

MATTIE STEPANEK

Born 1990 That Mattie Stepanek even lived to become a teenager and nickname his wheelchair Slick was inspiring enough without his also becoming a beloved bestselling poet. He was supposed to die soon after being born with the same rare form of muscular dystrophy that killed two older brothers and a sister before they were 4. But by that age the gregarious optimist was already conjuring up the bits of uplifting verse that were eventually collected in 2001's *Heartsongs,* the first of five books that together sold more than 1.5 million copies. "A heartsong is your inner beauty," explained the publishing sensation, a self-described "peacemaker" who was soon a regular on *Oprah* and corresponding with his hero, President Jimmy Carter (who spoke at Stepanek's Rockville, Maryland, funeral). "I could not believe," said Oprah, "that so much wisdom, so much power, so much grace, so much strength and love could come from one boy."

Stepanek wrote more than 2,000 poems. Their message: "We all have life storms. Play after every storm."

One of Sanford's last roles was with another squabbling TV family: playing herself on *The Simpsons.*

ISABEL SANFORD Born 1917

Leave *All in the Family* to go "movin' on up" to an untested spinoff called *The Jeffersons*? "I didn't want to go," admitted Sanford. "I like the sure thing." Understandable: She was the only one of her Harlem family's seven children to survive past infancy, and she was a single mother of three who struggled onstage before finally breaking through at 50 in the film *Guess Who's Coming to Dinner.* But as strong-willed Weezie Jefferson in TV's first series about an upscale black couple, she was a smash. "We bowed to her, she had that air," costar Sherman Hemsley said of the woman who became the first black actress to win a sitcom Emmy. "I was told many times to forget show business," said Sanford (whose health waned after neck surgery). "But I pursued it anyway. Voilà!"

MARGE SCHOTT, 75
The controversial, un-P.C. owner of the Cincinnati Reds was the first woman to buy and run a major league team.

PAUL WINFIELD, 62
The Oscar nominee (*Sounder*) launched a distinguished acting career after starring opposite Diahann Carroll on TV's *Julia.*

ROBERT PASTORELLI, 49
Best known as Eldin the Zen housepainter on *Murphy Brown,* the actor died of a heroin overdose.

J.J. JACKSON, 62
Among Earth's first VJs, he helped launch the fledgling MTV network in 1981.

JAN BERRY, 62
The coauthor of "Dead Man's Curve," the Jan and Dean leader was partially paralyzed in a 1966 auto accident at the height of his fame.

ALISTAIR COOKE, 95
The silver-haired, silver-tongued BBC correspondent hosted *Masterpiece Theatre* for two decades.

JUNE TAYLOR, 86
The choreographer's June Taylor Dancers brought balletic grace to TV's *Jackie Gleason Show.*

ELVIN JONES, 75
He was the wondrous drummer of John Coltrane's wondrous Quartet.

"I had always been a free spirit," said James, who regretted harm he had done to himself and others.

RICK JAMES Born 1948

In his guise as the Super Freak, the cartoonish rock and roll satyr that became his performing persona, he preened and prowled the stage in shrink-wrap spandex, wielding his bass like a power-funk-spewing fire hose and wailing his odes to kinky sex and excess. Before he was consumed by the lifestyle he celebrated in song—he did three years in the '90s for drug and sex crimes—James was a genre-leaping wunderkind. He proved equally at home performing with the Mynah Birds, the Canadian bar band he joined with Neil Young in the '60s, writing and arranging for the Temptations (his uncle was a founder) and winning a Grammy as cowriter of MC Hammer's hip-hop hit "U Can't Touch This." The Buffalo-born former choirboy completed his memoirs and a new album shortly before he died from an apparent heart attack. "Everything was falling into place for him," said son Ty. "He always said he felt he'd lived two or three lives. He was so fulfilled."

ANN MILLER

Born 1919 "I was never the star, I was the brassy, good-hearted showgirl," Miller conceded, but she held her own with such hoofing legends as Gene Kelly (*On the Town*), Bob Fosse (*Kiss Me Kate*) and Fred Astaire (*Easter Parade*), who called her "the fastest tap dancer in the world—I couldn't hold a candle to her."

Offscreen, the leggy Texan lived like a leading lady, seldom without a fur (she owned 54) or a man—she was divorced three times and dated billionaire Howard Hughes in between.

When movie musicals faded, she moved to Broadway, headlining a revival of *Mame* and earning a Tony nomination for *Sugar Babies* in 1980. Mickey Rooney, Miller's equally seasoned costar in the show, said before her death from lung cancer, "Nobody will ever tap-dance like her again."

Why get dolled up every day? "Because there are fans in the grocery store as well as the movie theater," she said.

"The only thing I'm depressed about is that I won't be able to share my death," Gray said in '87.

SPALDING GRAY Born 1941

In a lifetime of stories where no subject was off-limits, the famed monologuist foreshadowed his tragic final chapter. Diagnosed with bipolar disorder following a car accident in 2001, Gray attempted to take his own life at least twice before jumping from the Staten Island Ferry on a chilly January evening. Nearly two months later the father of two sons (aged 7 and 11) was found in New York's East River. "We talked about suicide," said his wife, Kathleen Russo. "It wasn't an option. He told me he had a responsibility to his children and me, and he would see it through." The Barrington, Rhode Island, native was the writer and performer of 17 monologues, including *Monster in a Box, Gray's Anatomy* and *Swimming to Cambodia,* a defining four-hour piece that was adapted into his most recognizable film. He began his career, however, in an eerily ironic way—with an improv performance that focused on the aftermath of his own mother's suicide.

RON O'NEAL Born 1937

It was the ultimate irony: The role that made him trapped him. Celebrated for his groundbreaking portrayal of street hustler Youngblood Priest in 1972's *Superfly,* O'Neal was an icon of the blaxploitation film era. While audiences associated him with his slick-haired, Cadillac-driving onscreen persona, the real O'Neal was a well-versed, award-winning actor who briefly attended Ohio State University and appeared in Off-Broadway revivals of *A Raisin in the Sun* and *A Streetcar Named Desire.* "The experience left me upset," he said before his death from pancreatic cancer. "Outside New York, people assumed I really was a hustler. *Superfly* took me from relative obscurity, but I haven't been offered that many roles since."

"The whole point of his character was to get out of that life," said O'Neal's wife, Audrey.

"He made small talk huge," said Merv Griffin, a Paar protégé and frequent guest host.

JACK PAAR Born 1917

"I have little or no talent," he said, "but I can be fascinating." The millions of viewers who tuned in religiously to *The Tonight Show* during his 1957-62 reign obviously agreed with that second assessment. Dick Cavett, then a *Tonight* writer, debunked the first, hailing Paar, who invented the format used by everyone from Johnny Carson, his successor, to Conan O'Brien, as a "quirky genius." Provocative and prickly, Paar often teared up on-camera and once walked off in the middle of a live broadcast after NBC censored a gag. The likes of JFK, Judy Garland and Woody Allen clamored to get on the show, not to plug but to converse. Overcoming a severe stutter to pursue a career in radio, the Ohio native followed *Tonight* with a failed variety series, then retired quietly with his wife and daughter. When Paar, who died of the effects of a stroke, was asked why he left *Tonight* so soon, he responded, "I never really had a good answer to that."

FRANCIS CRICK, 88 He helped discover the double-helix structure of DNA.

PAUL "RED" ADAIR, 89 An oil-field firefighter and folk hero, he inspired John Wayne's *Hellfighters.*

DAVID RAKSIN, 92 He scored the theme for *Laura* and more than 300 TV shows.

ELMER BERNSTEIN, 82 The Oscar winner's *The Magnificent Seven* theme popped up in everything from Marlboro ads to *Fahrenheit 9/11.*

AL DVORIN, 81 The announcer achieved immortality with his concert ender "Elvis has left the building."

DANIEL PETRIE, 83 The film director (*A Raisin in the Sun; Fort Apache, The Bronx*) later won Emmys for his work in TV.

ELISABETH KUBLER-ROSS, 78 The psychiatrist's *On Death and Dying* mined a surprisingly little-studied subject.

FRED EBB, 76 He and partner John Kander wrote the tunes for Broadway hits *Cabaret* and *Chicago,* among many others.

RUSS MEYER, 82 His low-budget, high-pulse sexploitation flicks like *Beyond the Valley of the Dolls* became cult classics.

MARVIN MITCHELSON, 76 The celeb divorce lawyer pioneered palimony for never-wed exes.

SKEETER DAVIS, 72 The Grand Ole Opry regular scored a plaintive pop hit in '63 with "The End of the World."

JOYCE JILLSON, 57 From working with stars to reading them, the *Peyton Place* actress became a widely syndicated astrologer.

GORDON COOPER, 77 The *Mercury 7* astronaut was one of the first Americans to orbit Earth.

LESTER LANIN, 97 He led the band at presidential inaugurals and the Charles/Di wedding.

VAUGHN MEADER, 68 The JFK satirist's 1962 LP *The First Family* sold 7.5 million copies.

HOWARD KEEL, 85 He starred in many MGM musicals (*Kismet, Kiss Me Kate*) and later in TV's *Dallas*.

OL' DIRTY BASTARD, 35 Rapper O.D.B. (né Russell Jones) was a founding member of the Wu-Tang Clan.

CY COLEMAN, 75 The Tony-winning composer brightened Broadway with *Sweet Charity, City of Angels* and scores more.

"I was the queen of the B's," rued Wray of her films. "If only I'd been a little more selective."

FAY WRAY Born 1907 For years she resented the big ape. And who could blame her? Wray had starred in Erich Von Stroheim's silent epic *The Wedding March,* was courted by novelist Sinclair Lewis and had worked with the likes of Gary Cooper, Cary Grant and Spencer Tracy. But she remains forever in our memories as the wispy beauty in the paw of the hairy beast King Kong. "It wasn't Shakespeare," she complained of the role in which her most memorable lines were nonverbal. "I yelled every time they said, 'Yell!'" Born in Alberta, Canada, she and her family migrated to the U.S. by stagecoach. Surviving three husbands (among them *It Happened One Night* screenwriter Robert Riskin, father of two of her four children), Wray titled her autobiography *On the Other Hand* and watched a screening of *King Kong* the day she died (of natural causes). By then, she conceded, "I realize it's a classic."

PETER USTINOV Born 1921

"He shows great originality, which must be curbed at all costs." There was no way the miffed London schoolmaster could contain the talents of Peter Ustinov. Where to start? Son of Russian émigrés, Ustinov was a satirist (first published at 14), actor (London stage debut at 18), playwright (*House of Regrets,* written at 19), author (of eight books) and jack of all Hollywood crafts. He wrote, directed, produced and starred in *Billy Budd,* collected two acting Oscars (*Spartacus, Topkapi*), an armload of Emmys and, oh yes, a Grammy (for his narration of *Peter and the Wolf*). Survived by his third wife and four children, Ustinov, who died of heart failure, was knighted for his artistic and humanitarian efforts. "The children of the world," said a U.N. Children's Fund executive, "have lost a true friend."

"He picked up voices like a blue serge picks up lint," a wag said of his skills as a mimic.

LAURA BRANIGAN Born 1957

The '80s disco diva who kept dance floors quaking to "Gloria" and "Self Control" could just as easily reduce revelers to tears with big, weepy electro-pop ballads like "Solitaire." "Early on I sang every song like it was my last breath on earth," she said. A onetime backup singer for Leonard Cohen, she went solo in 1982. "I was knocked out by the power of her voice," said Ahmet Ertegun, who signed her to Atlantic. Branigan's career had begun to cool by the grunge era, when she dropped out to nurse her husband, Larry Kruteck, before his 1996 death from colon cancer. A brief 2002 comeback was put on hold while she cared for her Alzheimer's-suffering mother in her Long Island home. It was there the singer died in her sleep of a brain aneurysm (the affliction that also killed her father and his father). "She was a giving person," said Branigan's brother Mark. "She was certainly full of life."

Branigan aimed high: "I want to move people the way Edith Piaf did."

"Nothing was as much fun as working with him," said *Pillow Talk* costar Doris Day.

TONY RANDALL

Born 1920 The truly odd thing about him: Though established on Broadway and in a series of G-rated Hollywood sex comedies, Randall didn't hit it really big until he bombed on TV. "It never got out of the bottom 10," he said of *The Odd Couple*, his series with Jack Klugman that sank in the original ratings but went through the roof in reruns. Randall was so closely identified with fussy, fastidious Felix Unger that a quarter century after the show was canceled, fans on the streets and subways of New York City greeted him as Felix. "It was fun for the first 15 years," he said in a characteristic sardonic deadpan. A Tulsa native who overcame a stammer, he was as impeccable in his speech as he was elegant in his dress. Married for 54 years to his college sweetheart, who died childless, Randall, at 75, married 24-year-old Heather Hanlan. The couple's two children brought him, he said before his death following heart-bypass surgery, "the greatest joy I've ever known."

CAPTAIN KANGAROO Born 1927 In the warm and sunny domain where Captain Kangaroo held court, "every day [was] another be-good-to-mother day," the Grandfather Clock told stories as well as time, and the twinkle-eyed man in charge was everyone's favorite grandpa. "No matter what kid dramas you were dealing with, he'd always cheer you up," recalled *American Idol* judge Randy Jackson, enraptured by the soft-spoken man who played the Captain for more than three decades. A former NBC page who debuted on TV as *The Howdy Doody Show*'s Clarabell the Clown, Bob Keeshan said he based *Captain Kangaroo* on "the warm relationship between grandparents and children." The widowed father of three was a lifelong children's welfare advocate who abhorred violence on TV. Keeshan, who died of heart disease, "was just as kind" as his character, said series regular Dr. Joyce Brothers. "There was nothing fake about him."

"I have grown into the part," he said of the role he created at 28 wearing a gray wig.

YASSER ARAFAT   Born 1929 After a life-time of fighting for Palestinian statehood, Arafat died as he had lived—a man without a country. A figure of stunning contradictions who wore a holster on his hip and brandished an olive branch while addressing the United Nations, he was ultimately responsible for horrific acts of terror, including the massacre of Israeli athletes at the '72 Munich Olympics, yet later shared the Nobel Peace Prize for reaching an accord with the Israeli state he long vowed to destroy. Born in Cairo, he was sent to Jerusalem at 4 after the death of his mother. Unable to stop the intifada violence that erupted after his subsequent rejection of the Oslo pact with Israel, he spent his last years confined to his Ramallah compound in the West Bank. His wife, Suha, a 34-years-younger ex-staffer of the Palestine Liberation Organization, had moved with their daughter to Paris in 2000 and didn't see her husband until just before he was brought there for treatment in the last days of his life.

He rarely appeared in public without his checkered kaffiyeh, which he studiously folded into the shape of old Palestine.

JANET LEIGH   Born 1927 "I don't take showers," Leigh said about her preference for baths after spending seven days in a soggy, flesh-colored bodysuit shooting the chilling shower scene in Alfred Hitchcock's *Psycho.* It earned her a 1960 Oscar nod and ultimately overshadowed other fine performances in films like *Touch of Evil* and *Bye Bye Birdie.* There was also *Houdini,* in which she costarred with Tony Curtis, her husband of 11 years. For Leigh, who died of vascular disease, another high was appearing opposite their accomplished daughter in 1998's *Halloween H2O.* Her mom taught her, Jamie Lee said adoringly, never to be a prima donna.

"I was allowed to be a part of cinematic history," Leigh said of her role in *Psycho.* **"I'm very fortunate."**

"He wasn't like that in real life," said comedian Rita Rudner. "He was clever and smart and knew exactly what he was doing. And he was very sweet."

RODNEY DANGERFIELD

Born 1921 Like his Olympian belly flop in the 1986 flick *Back to School,* the Long Island-born Jacob Cohen did many a loop-the-loop between starting in stand-up at 19 and making his long-delayed big splash in his early 40s. During a 12-year hiatus selling aluminum siding and polishing his one-liners on weekends, he eventually channeled a critical mass of insecurity and rejection into the indelible lovable-loser persona dubbed Dangerfield. Success followed with the movie smash *Caddyshack,* packed rooms in Vegas and his own Manhattan club where he incubated talent like Roseanne Barr and Jim Carrey, and a happy second marriage to florist Joan Child. But when he died from complications of heart surgery, his Web site posted this joke of the day: "I get no respect from anyone. I bought a cemetery plot. The guy said, 'There goes the neighborhood.'"

LEGENDS OF THE LENS

From Avedon to Cartier-Bresson, the world lost six great masters of photography. They exposed the horror of war, defined glamor, showed us the beauty in the mundane and left a stunning legacy of our times

SHEDDING INHIBITIONS

"We were in the studio with designer clothes and makeup and jewelry," Nastassja Kinski recalled about a memorable gig with Avedon. "But he suddenly said, 'This is not happening for me.' He made a few phone calls, and before you know it we had a snake in the studio. He was probably the only person who could have told me to take my clothes off and lie on the floor with a snake—and I'd do it."

This sultry view of Kinski at 20 became a hot-selling poster of the early '80s.

RICHARD AVEDON Born 1923 The native New Yorker revolutionized fashion photography by cajoling the glamorous to drop their guard in outlandish settings, including an unlikely shoot in a circus for *Harper's Bazaar* in 1955. After snapping *Vogue* covers for 24 years, Avedon in 1992 became the first staff photographer of the until then picture-impaired *New Yorker,* moving beyond couture to cover the culture at large, from Hillary Clinton to Toni Morrison to Rudolf Nureyev's foot. While on assignment in Texas doing a photo-essay on the 2004 election, he died of a brain hemorrhage. Represented in many museum collections and a celebrity in his own right, the twice-married Avedon was the inspiration for the Fred Astaire character in the 1957 movie classic *Funny Face.*

"WAR WAS THE EVENT OF MY YEARS"

"I watched [the foreign minister] limp forward, his wooden leg tapping out his progress in the silence," Mydans said, describing the scene as he witnessed the Japanese surrender aboard the battleship *Missouri.* "He leaned on his cane, took off his top hat and stripped off his gloves, and for an instant seemed confused. As I watched this man, at what for him must have been a terrible moment, I suddenly felt all my pent-up wartime anger drain away, and compassion filled my heart."

CARL MYDANS

Born 1907 "Pictures lay at every glance, but never have I suffered more in getting them." For Mydans, a reporter and photographer who made magic with a typewriter or camera, covering World War II was personal. Imprisoned by the Japanese along with his LIFE correspondent colleague and wife, Shelley, he was released in time to record his captors' surrender. (She died in 2002.) "Long after I'm gone," said Mydans, a Boston native who also captured the horror of combat in Korea and Vietnam as well as the peacetime tragedies of poverty and assassination at home, "I want people to be able to see—especially to feel—what I have seen and felt."

East Germans hid their faces to avoid being identified while seeking aid in West Berlin in 1953.

Mydans recorded the impact of death in Dallas on a New York commuter train and a masterpiece of workers shoveling rice for starving Japanese in '49.

A frozen moment that shocked the world: Adams witnessed the shooting of a North Vietnamese guerrilla during the 1968 Tet offensive.

"I WASN'T OUT TO SAVE THE WORLD"

Photojournalist David Hume Kennerly called the Pulitzer Prize-winning photo (top) that galvanized the antiwar movement in the U.S. "one of about five great photographs of the 20th century that really changed history." But Adams accepted the South Vietnamese army general's justification that the victim had killed an army friend of his along with his wife and children. "How do you know you wouldn't have pulled the trigger yourself?" Adams later wrote.

EDDIE ADAMS

Born 1933 At the annual photojournalism workshops he hosted at his farm in upstate New York, Adams liked to tease his students by playing the grandee, arriving to great fanfare on a chair carried by faux footmen. But the pomp was a put-on. A New Kensington, Pennsylvania, native and Marine veteran, Adams established his famed credit line in combat from Korea to the Persian Gulf, enduring the heat and the mud and the fear along with the grunts whose courage and travail he chronicled. While he will be best remembered for the devastating photo shown above, he would have preferred his legacy to have been his 1977 essay on the plight of Vietnamese boat people. Adams's shots of the desperate refugees led to the decision to admit approximately 200,000 South Vietnamese to the U.S. As Adams told his students, "You never know how your pictures are going to affect other people's lives."

MODEL TREATMENT

"He was this smiley, wonderful man," says Paulina Porizkova. "He never, ever made anybody look bad." Scavullo's concern for his glamazon subjects proved heartbreaking in the case of one of his favorite muses, super-model Gia Carangi. When her rampant drug use led the fashion world to write her off, Scavullo fought to get her on a 1982 *Cosmo* cover, hoping it would spur her to get clean. Despite his best efforts, which included concealing her arms to hide the track marks, Gia fell deeper into addiction until her death from AIDS in 1986.

FRANCESCO SCAVULLO Born 1921

Yes, there were models before 1965, when he shot the first of his 300-plus *Cosmopolitan* covers, but it was his alchemy of styling and lighting that made them truly super. Known singularly as Scavullo to fashionistas, the son of a New York supper-club owner practiced snapping his sisters before advancing to *Vogue* and LIFE. "He pulled the best out of anybody," said *Cosmo* editor Helen Gurley Brown, "by making that person think she was just glorious." Wed briefly to model Carol McCallson, Scavullo in 1971 took on Sean Byrnes as his stylist and companion. Despite nervous breakdowns, he never retired and suffered a fatal coronary just before a CNN interview. His life, said Byrnes, "was work, work, work."

You confirmed your iconhood by sitting for Scavullo. His works ranged from a nude centerfold of Burt Reynolds to Madonna, 1985 (above), and Andy Warhol, 1983 (right).

1967 He captured a strikingly androgynous image of Liza Minnelli the year she wed Peter Allen.

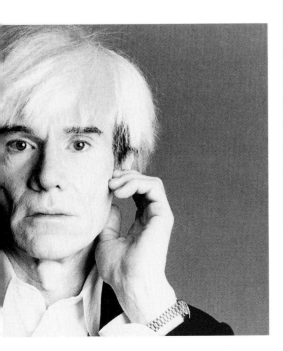

1981 Scavullo knew Brooke Shields long before this portrait with Calvin Klein. "Uncle Frankie," as she called him, shot her for an Ivory Soap ad at 11 months.

HENRI CARTIER-BRESSON
Born 1908 From the moment he bought his first Leica in 1932, the French photographer sought to capture what he termed "the decisive moment." Cartier-Bresson, who died at his home in Provence, leaves a treasure trove of social documents from the Spanish Civil War, the death of India's Mahatma Gandhi and Soviet society post-Stalin. Some of his most remarkable photographs were conceptually the simplest. His shots of everyday activities, like a man walking through a park or a child running an errand, uncovered the ineffable magic of life. While he left us classic portraits of personalities from Henri Matisse to Marilyn Monroe, the reticent lensman resisted having his own picture taken. "With him, France loses a genius photographer, a true master and one of the most gifted artists of his generation," said French president Jacques Chirac.

EYEWITNESS TO HISTORY

On January 30, 1948, Cartier-Bresson found himself in the middle of a tragic turning point in Indian history. He visited the tumultuous nation in 1947 and chronicled Mahatma Gandhi, its founding father, from afar at first before eventually arranging a meeting. During the introduction at Birla House in Delhi, Gandhi silently perused a small book of Cartier-Bresson photographs before stopping on a page showing poet Paul Claudel in front of a hearse. "What is the meaning of this?" he asked, before murmuring, "Death, death, death . . ." Fifteen minutes later, the Mahatma was assassinated.

An early scene in southern France, 1932.

A picnic on the bank of the Marne River, 1938.

The renowned shutterbug immortalized this moment of puppy love at a Paris outdoor cafe in 1959.

"My job as a portrait photographer is to seduce, amuse and entertain," said Newton, who shot Elizabeth Taylor at 52 in her L.A. pool in 1985.

NEWTON'S LAWS

"Most of my work is meant to be funny."

"My women always triumph."

"The nudes and bondage shots were my way of going beyond my own bounds."

"I think subjects pose so openly for me because I inspire confidence or because I'm older than most of them."

"Some people's photography is an art. Mine is not. If they happen to be exhibited in a gallery or a museum, that's fine. But that's not why I do them. I'm a gun for hire."

"You had to be this very powerful, in-your-skin, sexual woman," said a Newton model. Cindy Crawford (above in 1992) brought out what *Vogue*'s Anna Wintour described as his "naughty-boy sense of humor."

HELMUT NEWTON Born 1920

"I have made those nice ladies in pretty dresses look sexually available." That, in his own words, encapsules the Newtonian revolution in the previously prim world of fashion photography. Others called it simply a revolting development and labeled him the King of Kink. Moralists howled at his stark but highly stylized portraits of beautiful women on towering stilettos, stripped but strong, never coquettish and sometimes dangerous. When accused of misogyny, he responded, "Would I spend my life photographing something I hate? I think women become more powerful [in my photos] because they exude a great sexuality that will surely conquer the male. I think I'm a feminist." The son of a prosperous Jewish button manufacturer in Berlin, Helmut Neustadter fled in 1938 and settled in Australia, where he launched his career and found the love of his life, June Browne. A photographer herself, using the name Alice Springs, she was his constant model (and he hers) as well as his wife for 55 years until his death after a car crash in Los Angeles. "When he proposed to me, he did say that I would always be his second love, that photography would always be first," recalled Browne. "I thought that was marvelous."

FRONT COVER

Olsen: Armando Gallo/Retna; Spears: Reuters/Jive Records; Reagan: KRT/Abaca; Foxx: Paul Hawthorne/Getty; Lohan: Kathy Hutchins/Hutchins; Law: John Hayes/Everett; Gibson: Munawar Hosain/Getty

BACK COVER

Lopez: Jen Lowery/London Features; Kidman: Hahn-Khayat-Nebinger/Abaca; Usher: James White/Corbis Outline; Bush: Kevin Lamarque/Reuters/Corbis; Brando: Everett

TABLE OF CONTENTS

2-3 Mary Ellen Mark

BEST & WORST OF THE YEAR

4-5 Jason Reed/Reuters; Justin Lane/EPA **6-7** Martin Schoeller/Corbis Outline; Zuma **8** Ronald Asadorian/Splash News **9** Sue Ogrocki/AP **10-11** Jacqueline Bohnert/Contour; Troy Word **12-13** (from top left) V. Summers/Admedia; Courtesy Apple; Tammie Arroyo/AFF; Rose M. Prouser/AP/CNN; Giulio Marcocchi/Sipa; Jennifer Graylock/AP; Karwai Tang/Alpha/Globe; Lionel Cironneau/AP; Debra L. Rothenberg/Filmmagic; Bryan Bedder/Getty **14-15** Tim Shaffer/Reuters; Timothy A. Clary/AFP/Newscom **16-17** Lester Cohen/Wireimage; Nick Cornish/Rex USA **18-19** Arleen Ng/EPA; Sony/AP **20-21** Donald Miralle/Getty; Andrew Ross/Nunn **22-23** (clockwise from left) Lawrence Lucier/Filmmagic; Flynet; Ramey; Gary Hershorn/Reuters/Corbis; Jamie McCarthy/Wireimage; Anthony Harvey/Abaca **24-25** Eric Ogden; Glenn Weiner/Stargaze **26-27** Chris Pedota/Abaca; Matthias Clamer/Corbis Outline **28-29** Daniel Stier; Ben Margot/AP **30-31** (from left) Jeffrey Mayer/Starfile (2); Annamaria Disanto/Wireimage; Matt Baron/BEImages

DECISIVE MOMENTS

32-33 EPA/Landov; Rick Bowman/AP; Tony Avelar/AP **34-35** Courtesy *The New Yorker* (2); Newscom **36-37** Anatoly Zhdanov/EPA; Douglas C. Pizac/AP; Hacking Family **38-39** AP; Greg Lovett/*Palm Beach Post*/Zuma **40-41** Chris Usher; J.J. Guillen/AP **42-43** Joshua Lutz

WOW VOWS

44-47 John Solano; Invitation: Jonathan Alcorn/Wireimage **48** Lara Porzak **49** ABC; Simone & Martin **50** Maring Photography **51** Gruber Photography **52-53** Joe Buissink; X17; Steve Dennett/Splash News

SPLIT DECISIONS

54-55 Tsuni/Gamma **56** Tammie Arroyo/AFF **57** (from top) Rossa Cole/Splash News; Jon Kopaloff/Filmmagic **58** (from top) Courtesy Mattel; Janet Gough/Celebrity Photo **59** Alex Berliner/BEImages **60-61** Scott Jones; Tammie Arroyo/AFF

STORK TALES

62-63 Steve Sands/NY Newswire; Kevin Mazur/Wireimage ("Our proceeds from this photograph go to charity. It is our wish that by making this photograph available, we will protect the privacy of our daughter by discouraging unwanted pursuit by photographers —Courteney & David") **64** (from top) Wireimage; Denise Truscello/Wireimage **65** Lara Porzak **66-67** (from left) Kate Lilienthal/Splash News; Ben Evanstad/Bauer-Griffin; Steve Shaw; Joe Libonati; Kevin Mazur/Wireimage

BEST & WORST DRESSED

68-69 Carlo Allegri/Getty; **70-71** Lisa Rose/JPI; Hahn-Khayat-Nebinger/Abaca; Karwai Tang/Alpha/Globe; Jeff Kravitz/Filmmagic; Carlo Allegri/Getty; Russell Einhorn/Splash News **72-73** Splash News; Fitzroy Barrett/Globe; Steve Granitz/Wireimage; Carlo Allegri/Getty; Lisa Rose/JPI; Kika Press **74-75** Carlo Allegri/Getty (2); Lucy Nicholson/Reuters; Carlo Allegri/Getty (2); Gregg Deguire/Wireimage **76-77** Lawrence Lucier/Filmmagic; Peter Kramer/Getty; Adam Nemser/Photolink; Nancy Kaszerman/Zuma; Stephen Trupp/Star Max; Peter Kramer/Getty **78-79** Jon Kopaloff/Filmmagic (2); Mirek Towski/DMI; Francis Specker/Landov; Jean-Paul Aussenard/Wireimage; Mark Mainz/Getty **80-81** Peter Kramer/Getty; UK Press; Cosima Scavolini/Zuma; J. Graylock/JPI; Axelle/Bauer-Griffin; INF/Goff **82-83** G.S. Weiner/Stargaze; Gregg Deguire/Wireimage; Axelle/Bauer-Griffin; Stewart Cool/Rex USA; Lisa Rose/JPI; Wenn/Landov

GOOGLE

84-85 (from top) Logo courtesy Google™; AP; Vince Talotta/*Toronto Star*/Zuma; Kevin Mazur/Wireimage; Charles Rex Arbogast/AP; Phatphotos; Nikos Paraschoas/EPA/Landov

SCREAM

86-87 (from left) Sidsel De Jong/AFP/Getty; Reuters (2); Boone County Jail; Reuters; Mylan Ryba/Globe **88-89** (clockwise from top left) Andrea Renault/Globe; Jay L. Clendenin/Polaris; Wilfredo Lee/AP; Jon Kopaloff/Filmmagic; Paul Sancya/AP (2); Jeff Vespa/Wireimage; Spencer Green/AP; Louis Lanzano/AP; Dave Cruz/*Arizona Republic*/AP; Sergio Cortez/Wireimage

KEEPING IT REAL

90-91 (clockwise from left) © ABC; © FOX (2); © ABC (2); © FOX; © ABC (2) **92-93** (from left) Michael O'Neill; © CBS; Len Irish; © FOX; Robert Voets/© FOX

NEW KIDS

94-95 © ABC 2004 (2); **96-97** © HBO/2004; © FOX **98-99** (clockwise from left) Michael Caulfield/Wireimage; © 20th Century Fox; © Disney/Pixar; Ellis Parrinder; Chris Buck/Corbis Outline

THAT'S A WRAP

100-101 © Warner Bros.; Jim Cooper/AP **102-103** (from left) © HBO; © CBS/2004; © ABC (6); © NBC/Globe

TRIBUTES

104-105 Harry Benson; Bryan Chan/AP **106-107** (from left) Dirck Halstead/Getty; CBS Archive/Getty; Michael Evans/Zuma; EPA; Nana Productions/Sipa **108-109** Lori Stoll/Retna **110-111** (from left) Corbis Outline; Corbis Bettmann; MPTV; Rick Diamond/Wireimage; Corbis Bettmann; MPTV **112-113** Sid Avery/MPTV **114-115** (from left) Hulton Archive/Getty; Ralph Dominguez/Globe; Zuma; Everett (2); Retna; Everett; CNN; Photofest **116-117** (from left) Timothy Greenfield Sanders/Corbis Outline; A&E Network; Ken Regan/Camera 5 **118-119** (from left) Henry Grossman/Time Life/Getty; Janette Beckman/Retna; WGBH-TV **120-121** John Ficara/Gamma; Ken Whitmore/MPTV **122-123** Redferns/Retna; MPTV **124** Susan Johann/Corbis Outline **125** Globe (2) **126-127** Photofest; Patrick Swirc/Corbis Outline **128-129** (from left) Henry Diltz/Corbis; © ABC Photo Archive; © CBS Photo Archive **130** Gamma; Everett **131** © NBC/Globe **132-133** Richard Avedon; Inset: Marc Royce/Corbis Outline **134-135** Carl Mydans/Getty (3); Inset: Alfred Eisenstadt/Time Life/Getty; Eddie Adams; Inset: Polaris **136-137** Francesco Scavullo (4); Inset: Jack Chuck/Corbis Outline **138-139** Henri Cartier-Bresson/Magnum (3); Inset: Magnum **140-141** Helmut Newton/H&K/CPi (2); Inset: Galella

WORD UP

144 (clockwise from top right) Stephen Fuller; Corbis; Alamy; David Rams; Volker Mohrke/Corbis; Splash News; Wendy Grossman; NBC/*Saturday Night Live*; Taylor David Lewis/Keate; Jim Rogash/Wireimage

WORD UP

Maybe these pop-culture catchphrases had a short shelf life, but that didn't keep us from using them beyond the expiration date

HE'S JUST NOT THAT INTO YOU
Greg Behrendt, coauthor of the book by the same name

WARDROBE MALFUNCTION
Explanation of Janet Jackson's Super Bowl demo

ACID REFLUX
Excuse for Ashlee Simpson's *Saturday Night Live* snafu

Political-ad mantra of the year

VOTE OR DIE!
P. Diddy

LOW CARB
Marketing gimmick of the year

I'M ALL IN
Celebrity Poker

TELL ME WHAT YOU DON'T LIKE ABOUT YOURSELF
Plastic surgeons on *Nip/Tuck*

WHO'S YOUR DADDY?
Yankees fans to Boston pitcher Pedro Martinez

How Jon Stewart describes the Iraq situation on *The Daily Show*

SHAKE IT LIKE A POLAROID PICTURE

OUTKAST

FLIP-FLOPPER
George Bush describing John Kerry

BOYAKASHA
The Ali G. Show

It's a lot of pressure. I hope I don't build the building crooked.

Apprentice winner Bill Rancic, on overseeing the construction of a 90-story tower for Donald Trump

It was very uncomfortable up

Jennifer Lopez was married over the weekend. And she married salsa heartthrob Marc Anthony. No date has been set for the divorce. David Letterman

Everything I could hear in a trial, I've already heard on my show.

Oprah Winfrey, on being selected as a juror for a murder case

[Kabbalah] helps you confront your fears. Like if a girl borrowed my clothes and never gave them back and I saw her wearing them months later, I would confront her. Paris Hilton

How many points does a three-point field goal account for in a basketball game?

Test question on the final exam for the Coaching Principles and Strategies of Basketball course taught at the University of Georgia by the coach's son, who later lost his job

The camp is like an old-fashioned college campus— without the freedom, of course.

Martha Stewart, in a posting on her Web site, about life at the Alderson Federal Prison Camp

Janet was facing the other way. My side of the crowd didn't enjoy anything. Adam Sandler, on Janet Jackson's Super Bowl flash

Obviously, it's not

If things go right, I'll be there about a week, and if things don't go right, I'll be there about an hour and a half.

Rodney Dangerfield, before heart surgery, six weeks before he died

Apples are so sweet and they're wholesome. . . . Then she was born, and it became an international outrage. Gwyneth Paltrow, on naming her baby Apple